IMPACT OF SOCIAL MEDIA
ON
PEACE AND SECURITY

Dedicated to
Chief Architect of Indian Constitution
Dr. Babasaheb Ambedkar who started ***"the Mooknayak",***
on 31st January 1920 that changed millions of people's life

IMPACT OF SOCIAL MEDIA ON PEACE AND SECURITY

Prof. (Dr.) Vijay S. Khare

PENTAGON PRESS LLP

Impact of Social Media on Peace and Security
Prof. (Dr.) Vijay Khare

First Published in 2021

ISBN 978-93-90095-25-4

Published by
PENTAGON PRESS LLP
206, Peacock Lane, Shahpur Jat
New Delhi-110049
Phones: 011-64706243, 26491568
Telefax: 011-26490600
email: rajan@pentagonpress.in
website: www.pentagonpress.in

Printed at Aegean Offset Printers, Greater Noida, U.P.

Contents

Preface

This book focuses on Impact of Social media on Peace and Security. In the era of 21st century Social media has become one of the most widely accepted technological revolutions. It is not only became a technological invention but also a social communication norm in developed and developing countries. Social media has both positive and negative impacts on society which has been discussed in this book thoroughly. Primarily, social media refers to the internet based applications that empower people to communicate and exchange the resourceful information. Some crucial epitomes of social media are Blogs, Discussion Forum, Chat Rooms, Wikis, YouTube Channels, LinkedIn, Facebook, and Tweeter and so on and these tools can be accessed from mobile, computer and cellular phones.

The book is a result of an International Conference on Impact of Social Media on Peace and Security organised by the Department of Defence and Strategic Studies (DDSS), Yashwantrao Chavan National Centre of International Security and Defence Analysis (YC-NISDA) and Department of Ambedkar Studies, Savitribai Phule Pune University in collaboration with Indo-European Education Foundation (Poland), University of Applied Science, Nysa, (Poland), University of Galati (Romania) and Strategic Culture and Security Foundation, (Pune) on 7-8 March, 2019.

Evolution of social media and its relevance in present time needs to be understood as it has taken a stronghold in today's society and its use has become very common among the people in their day to day lives. Since the beginning of social media provides a varied opportunity to express thoughts, interact with one another and exchange the information worldwide. By providing such platforms to be familiar to the world at the same time causes a huge challenge to the national security.

In the contemporary world, social media has been changing its nature drastically has both positive and negative impacts, creates rooms to spread bitterness in the society in the form of fake news and intense rumours ultimately affects the Global Peace and Security.

This book incorporates a fruitful discussion on positive and negative impact of social media on Peace and Security. Articles published in this book leave us to think about an impact of social media on Peace and Security in an extensive manner. This is the need of hour to understand the pros and cons of social media which is largely affecting the Global Power and Politics. Hence, to understand the aspects of Social Media and its direct linkages to the Global Peace and Security, Department of Defence and Strategic Studies has organised an International Conference on **Impact of Social Media on Peace and Security**.

By organising such International Conferences on current issues like 'Impact of Social Media on Peace and Security', department has always tried to establish a linkage with current scenario in India and across the globe.

This book is consists of fifteen research articles by eminent professors and research scholars presented in the International Conference which was held on 7-8 March, 2019. Each article provides a diverse understanding about Social Media and its Impact on Peace and Security.

Dr. Vijay Khare elucidates that social media has widely become a critical tool for various international actors which include Governments, Civil Society and Terrorist groups. The author further argues Social media and technology has made the diplomacy more accessible to public and despite influencing all spheres of life, it largely impacts the foreign policy making process of a country. To understand the usage of social media by different groups and stakeholders the author has conducted a survey and made recommendations based on the collected information which includes issues concerned to social media and developing mechanism to keep check on activities threatens to national security.

Dr. Anna Opalka identifies the challenges, opportunities and factors which are needs to be taken into consideration such as university's information policy makers in order to educate and secure the future generations from manipulation and communication chaos because universities worldwide cannot ignore use of social media to communicate and create information directed to various stakeholders. She has adopted comparative analysis and synthesis, generalisation and systematisation along with empirical research method in this study.

Dr. Ecaterina Daniela Zeca argues that social media has become sophisticated toolkit in the contemporary world which acts as an online communication channel to share information, interact and collaborate but information scarcity, information abundance and distorted information are all equally dangerous which can lead to uncomfortable consequences. She further describes social media as not only confined to "like" and "unlike," but a high standards of ethics and accountability vital to positive outcomes.

Dr. Iryna kramar stresses on the importance of social media use in terms of security in different spheres of life. It also analyses social media users from the age perspective to define the main age group of people which is essential to understand importance of social media user's age as specifically, youth in this case, seen as the moving force for internationalisation and globalisation in the nearest future. The author further states that youth are considered as either passive or uninterested actors or as groups at high risk yet an active asset to promote peace, development and security.

Bartlomiej Kozak describes the advantages and disadvantages of recruitment of employees through social media and implications of being outside of network on professional development, employment opportunities and economic security. He shows how social media has become an important part of our lives which affects our actions and decisions and shape our everyday lives.

Dr. Pradeep Kumar and Daria Szczepańska expresses that social media affects people differently which depends upon pre-existing conditions and personality traits. The authors argue internet hoaxes have been around since the advent of the World Wide Web itself but a few had negative impacts. Recently, such hoaxes have transformed into 'fake news'. They give example of current coronavirus pandemic which was started in a laboratory in China to kill millions and misinformation caused people to act erratically and dangerously and social media platforms, such as Facebook, were played a big role.

Dr. Sushama Bhosale emphasises on impact of social media on social behaviour and argues that social media has brought change in social norm, affects on perception, social behaviour and lifestyle of youth and also helping to borrow the social foreign culture. The author also demonstrates that all the participants do not agree or are undecided about the construct of posting of irrelevant racist abusive anti-cultural and religious contents and links, promotes hatred among racial groups in the society while using social media.

Dr. A. Thennarasu claims that the world has been facing a new kind of warfare which is not fought in the battlefield but in the various spheres of social media as conflicts today turned internationalised and not remained localised. The author quotes, Alvin Toffler, who says the full implications of what we termed 'third wave knowledge warfare' have not yet been digested. The wars of the future will increasingly be prevented, won or lost based on information superiority and dominance. In this context, he recommends separate wing in the Indian Armed Forces to tackle social media related attacks on India's national security because it lacks comprehensive national cyber security strategy to counter the cyber threats posed by adversaries through Social Media.

Dr. Biswajit Mohapatra describes introduction of 'new media' particularly internet would reduce the amount of time individuals spend on existing 'old media'. He argues evolution of new media technologies are responsible for the globalisation to occur. Besides, it has become a great interest for global espionage putting individuals and the countries to a greater risk, demands to improve governance within the country and establish close coordination with other national and international agencies to track down malicious activities and enhance national security.

Dr. M.L. Sali defines the comprehensive nature of security and emphasises how social media has relevance to security in wider perspective. To study the linkages of National Security and social media he has used analytical approach. He elucidates there are numbers of challenges and problems emerged through the negative use of social media and terrorism is one of them flourished globally. Besides, internet security has also increased due to social media and helped to develop criminalisation tendency in the society.

Dr. Saeideh Shariati Najafabadi focuses on how media development policies and programs can help to prevent insecurity and violent conflict and contribute towards marinating peace. She suggests each conflict must be understood in the context of its own political, social and cultural aspects since it is multidimensional and complex in nature. Also, impartial and inclusive media which gives voice to people from all sections of societies, including the most marginalised, can be an instrument of peace and security.

Dr. Gunratna Sontakke evaluates the impact of fake news, campaigns and political propaganda through social media and examines methods and techniques used to spread misinformation and its implications on society. He opines people should be educated how to spot fake news and not to believe it and spread it. They should be educated to validate or verify the news with authentic sources and government should bring laws and regulations to counter such activities.

Col. Arunender Thakur contends that a social platform in civilised societies has originated way back in our civilisation by giving the references of sacred scriptures. By highlighting the positive and negative aspects of social media he argues that the confidential messaging system has been followed since Vedic period as Confidentiality, Integrity and Security of the messages were significant but now time has changed which has transformed the world and under the progress of social media which is associated with advanced technologies tries to encircle and threaten the very purpose of our existence.

Mr. Milad Ghiasi analyses the effects of peer pressure in social media on people's behaviour, peace and security. He shows peer pressure in social media has influenced the youth in massive way. He further argues people who are responsible, sensible and successful can be a positive influence hence the message of peace and other noble causes can be spread among people through the social media and Internet world wide.

Dr. Surendra Kamble argues that border dispute between India and China has taken social media to a new height. Also, coverage of Indian newspapers and television channels are still dominated by the issue of border skirmishes and Chinese intrusions over Indian Territory. In addition, people through social media raised their voices as far as China-India border dispute is concerned which influences the Indian government's policy making unlike China where Chinese media gives narrative and agenda and narrows it down and shapes its foreign policy through decision-makers. Moreover, the author has conducted a survey on use of social media as well as analysed China-related editorials of Indian newspapers include *The Times of India, The Hindu, The Indian Express, The Economic Times and The Financial Express.* The survey finds border issue as dominating factors in the editorials but plea for mutual trust and closer economic ties between the two countries are also growing at the same time by considering China's economic growth and its role in the global affairs.

I would like to record my sincere thanks and gratitude to the eminent contributors who have presented their papers in the International Conference. The publication of this research articles would not have been possible without the encouragement and support of the Hon'ble Vice-Chancellor, Prof. (Dr.) N.R. Karmalkar and all university authorities who are continuously supporting for this important task.

Finally, I thank the teaching and non-teaching staff of the DDSS, Dr. Ravi Thorat, Dr. Deepali Khaire, Dr. Anjani Devi, Mr. P.J. Khache, Mr. Gavrav Kokil, Dr. Sushma Bhosale, Dr. Savita Patil, Ms. Raisa Chaudhary, Ms. Bharati Kokil, Dr. Dimple Chaudhary, Mr. Balaji Kambale, Ms. Shivani S. Singh, Mr. Satish Gadadare, Mr.Gaurav Kokil, Mr. Onkar Sonwane, Mr. Sagar Gaikwad, Ms. Sheetal Jagtap, Mr. Dnyaneshwar Gaikwad, Mr. Vijay Mohad, Mr. Ganesh Shinde, Mr. B. Munnuswami and all serving officers, who are students and research scholars in the department who helped us a lot in completing this book.

I am thankful to Mr. Rajan Arya and his team from Pentagon Press LLP for bringing out the book within the shortest possible time. I hope that the readers will find out our efforts worthy and the book will serve the expected needs.

Prof. (Dr.) Vijay Khare

About the Contributors

Prof. (Dr.) Vijay Khare is former Dean, Faculty of Humanities, Savitribai Phule Pune University, SPPU (formerly University of Pune). Prof. (Dr.) Vijay Khare is also the Director of the International Centre, SPPU. As the Director of the International Centre, he provides excellent leadership to all international engagements. He is a Professor and the Head of the Department of Defence & Strategic Studies, SPPU. He was awarded the Post Doctoral Fellow by UGC. He holds M.Sc. and Ph.D. from Pune University. Dr. Khare is a recipient of the prestigious Fulbright Fellowship, USA, awarded in 2017. Dr. Khare was awarded Erasmus Fellow by the European Commission in 2015. Dr. Khare's areas of expertise are national security, no-traditional security, terrorism and counter-terrorism, peace and conflict resolution and human rights. Dr. Khare holds a number of Administrative and Governance positions.

Dr. Anna Opalka, Head, External Relations Department and International Cooperation Office at UAS Nysa, Director of the Research and Development Centre for Conservation and Renovation, coordinator of the IEEF—Indo-European Educational Foundation branch in Nysa, Poland, university lecturer and personal trainer. Graduated in Economy of Real Estates and Investments at the University of Economics in Cracow, completed Management Postgraduates Studies at the University of Wroc³aw, certified ISO auditor and manager, European League Institutes of Arts Representative Board member. Previously also responsible for the University Promotion activities. In 1998-2004 staff member at the Silesian University of Technology in Gliwice at the International Cooperation and Research Offices. Anna Opalka has been a coordinator of many international projects under Erasmus+, Leonardo da Vinci, PHARE CBC, Europa Creativa. Culture 2000, international conferences and venues for last 20 years and also has an experience in building some virtual educational platforms in the area of conservation and culture heritage protection and management (RESELTAM and RESPECT Projects). Scientific area reflecting publications focuses on the international educational and research projects management in the areas of academic internationalisation, and cultural heritage protection and management.

Dr. Ecaterina Daniela Zeca is graduated in Economics and Engineering, Computer Peripherals; holds a Doctoral degree in Economics and Postdoctoral studies in Bio-economy and Sustainable Development and Marketing (Romanian Academy). The activity is carried out in the field of fundamental analysis and applied research in marketing management, oriented towards generating new knowledge, substantiating and supporting policies and strategies for sustainable development. Dr. Ecaterina Daniela Zeca is founder of European Research Centre for Marketing and Agrilnd, CDEAMIA. She is able to offer constructive challenge. Dr. Zeca contributed with innovative ideas and research works on: Sustainability/New European Lifestyle and Youth Unemployment/ Future of the European Union: Europe in Transition, Youth Unemployment. She was a Keynote speaker at International Strategic Research Congress 28th Sept, 2017, KEMER—Turkey; Organizer, coordinator, moderator both of International Workshop "Globalization Remodels the Way We Live, Relate to One Another, Work and do Business" and of "The International Conference". UGAL International Conference Multidisciplinary HUB for the Higher Education Internationalization by Means of Innovative Interaction with the Labor Market and Society, October, 2018, Galati, Romania. Some of Dr. Zeca's thoughts and ideas about Higher Education are expressed here: The Information Economy. Formal Training, Adapted to the Nomadic and Ubiquity of Information, E-Labour Platforms Streamlining the Process Right Person For Right Job (International Conference New Trends in Sustainable Business and Consumption, Germany), JITG Just in Time Graduates, and Shifting Academic Model (ASM Pune, India, Jan 2018); The Global Higher Education Market (GHEM), Perfectly Competitive

Educational Market and Entropy Concepts (International Conference, Melbourne, Australia).

Dr. Iryna Kramar: Professor at the Department of Economics and Finance Ternopil Ivan Puluj National Technical University (TNTU), she is Doctor of Science (in Economics). Field - "Economics and enterprises management (by the types of economic activity)". Head of Indo-European Centre (IEC) at TNTU (representative of IndoEuropean Education Foundation, Poland (IEEF). Dr. Iryna is Scholar of the Cabinet of Ministers of Ukraine - she received Scholarship for Young Researchers. She has been awarded the State Award of the Ukrainian Parliament. She is Member of joint international project «The Centre of Competence on Entrepreneurship and Business Education" between Estonian Business School and Ternopil Business School supported by the Ministry of Foreign Affairs of Estonia. Dr. Iryna is Former Vice-dean of Foreign Students Department, TNTU. She has authored of more than 100 scientific papers and organized more than 70 scientific and cultural events for students and researchers. Dr. Iryna is recipient of more than 20 awards from the city council, regional council, TNTU and students.

Bart³omiej Kozak: He graduated Managerial Postgraduate Studies in Company Management at the University of Economics in Wroclaw. He did Master of Science in Computer Science from the University of Technology in Wroc³aw and IT engineering from the University of Applied Sciences in Nysa. Kozak has been a professional advisor for 12 years and is involved in development of startups and academic business incubators. He studies the labour market and the impact of its development on young people and their economic security.

Dr. Pradeep Kumar holds a doctor degree in Economics, double master degrees-Executive MBA, and M.A. in International Relations (University of Warsaw), and Bachelor in Laws-L.LB. 5years (BVP's NLC, Pune, India). Dr Kumar is a keen researcher and academician in the area of International Business and Legal practices with 11 years of academic work experience in the area of teaching, training, research, and business development. He is responsible for institution building activates, collaborations, faculty development & trainings, quality enhancement in the higher education and capacity building initiatives for students, scholars and business elites. Since 2008, Dr Kumar is working to develop relations between India and Poland based on academia—Industry interlinked model of business cooperation and supporting various universities in Poland, India and other European Union member states. He has presented a new model of business cooperation for Polish universities in order to get well qualified Indian students through "CET-India Test", which helped many universities in Poland and numbers of Indian students studying in Poland has been increased up 5000 in 2018 comparing from 209 in 2014.

Dr. Sushama Bhosale is working as Principal at Mamasahib Mohol College, Paud Road, Pune. She is M.A. Ph.D. SET, Erasmus Mundus Postdoctoral Fellow. Since last 25 yrs. She is teaching Psychology for UG&PG. She is Ph.D. guide for Psychology for Savitribai Phule Pune University & North Maharashtra University, Jalgaon. She is working as a Career Counsellor, for Eltis and Sifil Institute of Symbiosis International University, Pune, from 2007. She has received two fellowships, namely, Post-Doctoral Fellowship awarded by European Commission Experts Asia—Erasmus Mundus 2015-2016 and Fellowship awarded for Ph.D. under Faculty Development Programme of UGC from 2008-2010 She has published 5 books which are, "A Heart Study", a book written in English, published in Germany and four books published by Sakal publication. Dr. Bhosale has published more than 30 research articles in International and National journals. She chaired a session and conducted workshop on "Rational Emotive Behaviour Therapy at Yale University, USA& Masaryk University, Czech Republic. International Center of Savitribai Phule Pune University. She prepared modules for Health Center, Savitribai Phule Pune University. She is working as a resource person for Extra Mural Activity and Soft Skill Center, Dr. Bhosale also has to her credit more than 450 articles in Daily Sakal; 105 articles in Daily Prabhat; 20 articles in Marathi magazine "Menka". She is also associated as resource person for SAAM TV, Jai Maharashtra and 9TV channels.

Dr. A. Thennarasu has been former chairperson, School of Political and International Studies, Professor and Head (Retd) Department of Defence and Strategic Studies, and Professor and Head In-charge Dr. Ambedkar Centre for Economic Studies, coordinator, Masters and M. Phil programmes and Chairman Drafting Committee of Curriculum Development (2006-2016). Prof. A. Thennarasu was a Member of Syndicate (Governing Body) (2006-2009) and also was Member of Senate and Academic Council of University of Madras. He was a Chancellor's nominee to the Senate of Madurai Kamaraj University 2007-2010. He was a chairman of Board of Studies in Defence and Strategic Studies and Nautical Sciences, University of Madras &Member of Board of Studies in Bharathiar University Coimbatore and Thiruvallur University Vellore. Convener-Chairman, University Inspection Commission to National Defence College, New Delhi, Since 2012 Defence Services Staff College, Wellington since 1991, Officers Training Academy, Chennai since 2012, Prof. A. Thennarasu has more than 34 years of teaching, research and administrative experience. He has been a invited speaker-visiting professor to Defence Service Staff College since 1991. Prof. A. Thennarasu is a Member of Expert Committee for Defence and Strategic Studies, University Grants Commission, New Delhi, and also Member of confidential work of UGC, UPSC, TNPSC, Punjab Service Commission etc. He also invited speaker/visiting professor National Defence College New Delhi Since 2007.

Dr. Biswajit Mohapatra is an Associate Professor at the Department of Political Science, North-Eastern Hill University, Shillong, India where he also directs various research programmes in Politics and International Relations in the said University. He holds a Ph.D. in International Relations from the Jawaharlal Nehru University of India, a Master's degree in Political Science from the University of Delhi and Bachelor of Arts (Hons) in Political Science from Ravenshaw College, Cuttack, Odisha. Besides he has also attended the Advanced International Programme in Conflict Resolution (PACS) at the Department of Peace and Conflict Research at Uppsala University He has written two books,viz., and published extensively on International Relations and Look East/ Act East, South East Asia, China and North East India in peer reviewed journals both in India and abroad and have presented papers in various national and international seminars and conferences. He has also visited a number of foreign countries in connection with his academic assignments. His research interests include the political economy of India's Foreign policy & National Security; Asia-Pacific

Security; India, China & East Asia relations; Contemporary Territorial and Maritime disputes; Regional Economic integration. His personal Profile is available at http://nehu.academia.edu/BiswajitMohapatra

Dr. M. L. Sali is Principal, M.V.P's, Arts & Commerce College, Taharabad Tal. Baglan Dist. Nashik. Dr. Sali completed his M.A., M. Phil. and Ph. D. in Defence and Strategic Studies, University of Pune. He has teaching experience of 22 Years U.G. and P.G. teaching experience at Bhonsala Military College, Nashik. Dr. Sali has been honoured by Five Awards given by the University of Pune for securing highest marks in Defence and Strategic studies at B.A. and M.A. level. He has wide experience in Research and Guideship. Dr. Sali is a member of Board of Studies (BOS), University of Pune and North Maharashtra University, Jalgaon & worked as an Adhoc Board member B. Ambedkar Marathwada University and also Aurangabad. He is a Faculty member of Mental, Moral and Social Sciences, University of Pune. Dr. Sali also Participated in restructuring of New syllabus in various Universities of the Country. Dr. Sali is working as a "Principal" since 2010 & organized numbers of seminar, Workshop and Events. He has delivered lectures, as a, "Resource Person", at various colleges, Universities & UGC Refresher Courses. As a Principal, Dr. Sali appeared the process of Accreditation: NAAC Peer team visited his college i.e. K.R.T. Arts & Commerce College, Vani Dist. Nashik during 2013 & M.V.P's, Arts & Commerce College, Taharabad Tal. Baglan Dist. Nashik, during October-2017.

Dr. Saeideh Najafabadi is an Iranian is a Qualified Policy and Advocacy practitioner and scholar on gender issues and has been an advocate of gender equality on print and Social Media with over 20 years of experience in both organization and freelance levels. She has worked with different journals and magazines advocating women's rights since the age of 18. Dr. Saeideh also worked on quantitative and qualitative research reports on gender issues in Iran since 2013. She is experienced in organizing and conducting training on a wide range of gender issues and women's leadership. Dr. Saeideh completed her PhD in Political science (2012-2016) from the Centre for Central Eurasian Studies, University of Mumbai, India. She did her MA in International Relations (2007-2009) from the Islamic Azad University, Shahreza Branch. Dr. Saeideh is also a recipient of the Peace Fellow Certification on Conflict

Resolution and Peace-building Rotary Peace Center during the Conflict Resolution and Peace-building Professional Development Program, Chulalongkorn University, Thailand, January 2018-April 2018.

Dr. Gunratna Sontakke: Research Scholar at Department of Anthropology, Savitribai Phule Pune University.

Col. Arunender Thakur is an officer of Indian Army, serving in its Logistical arm. The Scholar has been associated with the Supply chain management of certain stores for Indian Army including Clothing, Armament, Ammunition, etc from various corners of the Country to different locations where required including inhospitable terrains. He has served in High Altitude, Counter Insurgency Operation Areas, Field Areas and all types of terrain in the country. He has also served as Instructor at the Premier learning Institution of Army, College of Materials Management Jabalpur. He has written various service related articles and has expertise in field of ammunition and related support system. At present he is Pursuing Research in Organisational interest at DDSS at SPPU and has interests in Vedic studies.

Mr. Milad Ghaisi is a PhD student in Psychology, Milad Ghiasi, an Iranian, Department of Psychology, Savitribai Phule Pune University, Pune, India. MA Clinical Psychology Graduated in 2015, from SPPU. Has experience of working as a Child Psychologist and Family Counsellor, also, conducted workshops/seminars with Indian, Iranian and international students, regarding Health Psychology, Family Counselling and Child Psychology. Active Member of Iran Association, regularly conducting workshops regarding Family Counselling, Child Psychology and Health Psychology. Also has experience of conducting workshops and giving speeches at the Culture House of the Islamic republic of Iran, Mumbai. Milad was awarded the prestigious recognition of Ambassador of Peace as an international student in Pune by the Times of India (Pune Times).

Dr. Surendra Kamble is Associate Professor at the Department of Defence and Strategic Studies S.P.D.M. College Shirpur affiliated to KBC North Maharashtra University Jalgaon.

1

Impact of Social Media on India's Foreign Policy

Dr. Vijay Khare

"The media is the most powerful entity on earth. They have the power to make the innocent guilty and to make the guilty innocent, and that's power. Because they control the minds of the masses."

— **Malcolm X**

Introduction

Over the last 30 years the nature of communication has undergone a significant change. Apart from this over the last few years, social media is the key source of government usage, education, business etc. If we look at the last few years, social media has become a way in which something is usually done with an online perspective where major social networks and social media websites make changes and improvements on a fairly regular basis. These websites offer a way of approaching a problem or making progress towards something through which we communicate with people. In education, social media is playing great and wide role. Email has a profound effect on the way we communicate with people. The communication is shorter and more frequent than letters which were the norm earlier. The response time has also diminished. Instant messaging has created another method of interaction, where the length of messages is shorter and the interaction is more conversational. For example, broadcast technologies like Twitter transform these shorter bursts of communications from one on one conversation to short news. Social media has the potential to fundamentally change the character of our social lives interpersonal and at a community level. Online communication tools are the main example, which have the potential to increase our awareness of the movements of our professional or social contacts. For example- Twitter, offers us an update of things people happen to be doing at a particular point of time. As social media has become more accessible, it has become a means by which people, non-state actors and even governments can share their foreign policy priorities in an effort to receive feedback, engage in diplomacy, educate people, and attempt to influence foreign policy process. Facebook, Twitter and YouTube created a greater sense of urgency among those who seek a greater understanding of the impact of social media on foreign policy.

Social media and foreign policy work can be found in different fields like public diplomacy which is conducted as part of the broader public diplomacy literature and also found in the political communication literature, in working papers and articles generated by foreign policy think tanks such as academic journals dedicated to area studies that often concentrate on specific episodes of social media used to influence foreign policy. Social media has become a critical tool for a wide variety of international actors running the complete range or scope of something from governments to portions of civil society to terrorist groups such as Al-Qaeda and the Islamic State of Iraq Syria (ISIS, also known as the Islamic State of Iraq and the Levant or ISIS based in part on the group's territorial claims).

Social media and foreign policy are explored across disciplines and start to deal with (a situation or problem) in a certain way. These are the desirable changes in area of theoretical development. Network theories focus on interactions between parts of a network (in this case a social network); network analysis methods are sometimes employed as part of this theoretical framework. Social media has made diplomacy more accessible to the public. Earlier the role of public remained as receptors but now through social media, they have become prominent actors. India has been focusing on technological advancement as it does not want to be left behind in the race for soft power using mediums of social media. Indian diplomacy is focusing on the true sense of communication, rather than one-way oration it has opened the gates for several actors. India's former Foreign Minister, Sushma Swaraj has made this possible.[1]

Methodology

To solicit the information about usage of social media and its tools, it was decided to conduct a survey of social media usage by different group of stakeholders. A list of stakeholders who use social media for various purposes was prepared and thirty stakeholders were selected for the pilot study. Social media is used by most of the students, teachers, researchers, media personnel, government officials and politicians etc. To test the group, a structured questionnaire designed for this purpose was distributed among these stakeholders and they were requested whether they have any difficulty in understanding the questions. They have been given sufficient time to think and fill in the questionnaire. The researcher did not receive any suggestions to modify the questionnaire. Hence, it was decided to distribute the questionnaire to all thirty stakeholders to conduct the pilot study. Nobody suggested any improvement to the questions asked to them. Questions were designed to keep in mind the objectives of the paper. There were twenty-five questions included in the questionnaire. To knows the views of various stakeholders who are using social media and social media tools, about the use of social media and its impact on Indian Foreign Policy, a structured questionnaire was developed and distributed to 550 participants which includes post graduate students, research scholars, defence officers, faculty members etc. Out of which we have received 484 responses from various groups of stakeholders.

Pilot Study Conducted

Nowadays social media is an essential part of life of users who know how to use the medium for various purposes. We have conducted a pilot study about the use of social media by students, researchers, faculty members etc. We have developed a structured questionnaire for this purpose and to test these questions from these users, a pilot study was conducted. The analysis of these questionnaires is given below: First six questions are about use of social media, social media tools, purpose of using social media tools, their participation and contributing views on India's Foreign policy through these tools and how they update their knowledge in Indian foreign policy etc. The stakeholders were asked whether they used social media networking and at what level. 31 per cent stakeholders answered they used social media for personal use, 28 per cent as students, and 11 per cent as research scholars and others are also using social media networking at different levels, but their percentage is low. Second question which was asked to them was which social media tools they used, Facebook was the most popular tool used by majority of people which is used by all and YouTube and Twitter were among the second most used by them. There are other tools like, LinkedIn, Blog, Slideshare, Instagram, Snapchat, MySpace and Flicker which were also used by a few students. In the questionnaire it was also asked for what purposes they used these social media tools. Five options were given to them. Out of which they mentioned that they use social media tools to obtain knowledge and information in various subject areas and for their personal use. Stakeholders also said that they use it for updating information and knowledge and also for their personal interest in the Indian foreign policy. It was further asked them whether their views on various problems or policies is contributed by them through social media tools. 17 per cent stakeholders said that they do contribute their views on international relations; views on national security etc and 11 per cent said that they were not contributing their views. 12 per cent stakeholders expressed their views on India's foreign policy through social media tools, 15 per cent said that they did not express their view, and here the percentage of negative is more than positive responses. It was further asked them whether they visit Govt. of India's Ministry of External Affairs website to get recent updates on India's foreign policy.

In response to this, 21 per cent said that they frequently visit the website and get updates. Another question asked was that many incidents happen in the country and whether these incidents force the government to frame the foreign policy. 76 per cent participants gave positive responses and mentioned that a few cases in which the government has decided the foreign policy for example in the Kashmir valley, new conditions of Kashmir valley is rules and accordingly, the government has changed policy with internal government of Kashmir as well as some border issues where terrorist attacks took place. It was further asked if foreign policy changes when the central government changes. In response to this, 22 (73 per cent) respondents said policy is slightly changed as per situation. 9 (30 per cent) said policy is completely changed in certain cases. Participants were asked whether use of social media tools could influence and affect our Indian foreign policy, out of 30 participants, 24 (80 per cent) said it could influence and affect it whereas 6 (20 per cent) gave negative responses. In the positive response, participants said that the reactions and feedback from citizens affect the foreign policy; few said that the media has a great impact on citizens in influencing our policy. Whereas one participant said that social media tools only gives information (may be true or false), but the ultimate decision lies with the government. Another person expressed that public opinion of Chinese presence in Doklam has influenced the government to not unilaterally withdraw forces from the region. It was further asked whether social media has been influenced by or has an impact on Indian national security and IFP. 17 (56 per cent) participants opined that it is influenced and has an impact because all the information is exchanged through social media, because of radicalization of people through social media which has made national security experts to track all social elements. Cyber security is a matter of great concern now that social media is very active and India should implement a cyber security mechanism. 6 (20 per cent) participants said there was no impact on security and FP. Twenty-three (76 per cent) respondents opined that present government is more active on social media as compared to the previous government and 2 (6 per cent) said they were not active and 5 (16 per cent) did not give their response. Few opinions are that the present government is fully active in social marketing because the previous government failed in connecting with the people that is the reason they were not elected in 2014. Another participant expressed that the present government is posting and tweeting on Twitter their views. Our Prime Minister Mr. Modi has one of the largest followers on Twitter, and the existing government advertisement uses all programs set up as new one on social media.

A question was also asked about China playing an important role in international power politics and how it is not actively involved on social media. However, 11 respondents said that it is actively involved social media whereas 10 participants said it is not. Nine respondents did not respond to this question. Some comments on this question are that even China plays an important role in international power politics, however, they do not expose itself or any information on social media which is an external step towards success, China tends to be self-sufficient by having their own social media sites. China has their own social media tools for domestic use and China is developing its human resources focus on technology which is used by social media, but the information provided is limited.

It was asked whether strategic think tanks influence foreign policy through social media. 14 participants replied positively yes whereas 11 participants replied negatively. Think Tanks work on the agenda of the government and think tanks give out performance views and not necessarily what is good for the government.

Social media reflects meaningful political competition over India's Foreign Policy, if so what relationship can social media reveal and its limitation of social media data for the use of research scholars. Only three participants said yes and six participants said no. Majority of the participants (21) did not respond to this question. Here available resources are shared on social media and they are provided to research scholars, but it has a limitation to some extent, without authenticity and the research scholar will drive it by data available on social media.

Further the participants were asked whether social media has an impact on the foreign policy, 20 participants replied positively while four denied. Since social media provides everyone a platform to voice their opinions, miscreants can easily sway public opinion over a certain issue by making false claims. Therefore, we can say that social media does play a role in the making of foreign policy.

Conclusion

Since 2004 there has been a widespread growth of the social media. Earlier, Facebook was the top ranked social networking site with around one million users. Slowly, the network began to enlarge and today it has more than around one billion registered users. Through the course of the research it has been proven substantially that social media has an impact and influence on all spheres of life. This includes its impact on foreign policy making in India and across the world. Social media has emerged as the top tool for gathering information and for disseminating information, not just by common citizens but also used by government agents and officials. The reason why social media has been used so extensively is its power of reach and time. It can spread information at the spur of the moment and among thousands of people at the same time. Traditional forms of media like the television or the news paper did not have such a huge impact on normal life like social media does. The Pew Research Center released the Social Media Update of 2014 in January 2015 which stated that around 71 per cent of the Internet users in the US are on Facebook. The Twitter audience rose by 27.7 per cent from 2013 to 2014. India has recorded the highest social networking growth of around 37.4 per cent in 2013. With a rapid expansion of social networking sites, India is expected to be the largest Facebook population country in 2016. Social media unites millions of people across the globe on a single platform. Apart from unity, the social media is also used by the politicians for the purpose of campaign during election. Likewise, it provides many other advantages.

The Impact of Social Media on Security Threats

Used by terrorists – Due to the easy availability and widespread use of social media, most of the terrorists use this medium to achieve their goals. Around 90 per cent of the organized terrorism on the Internet takes place through the social media. The terrorist groups spread their messages through the sites like You Tube, Twitter or Facebook and recruit people via them. For example, the terrorist group of ISIS spreads their messages and activities through the social media.

International users – The other national and international users such as the political parties, NGO's, hackers pose a serious threat using the social media. For example, during the civil turmoil in the Arab Spring Uprising, the various governments were threatened through the social media.

Communal Violence – With the help of social media, people have started attacking each other's religion on this platform by tweeter. Sensitive tweets regarding religion are becoming a common phenomenon. Circulation of certain pictures and videos through social media also creates a panic situation among the masses. This is a threat to the internal security of the nation as it disturbs the communal harmony and increase tension of the existing government and public also.

Threat to internal security – With the advent of social media, issues like economics, media and science are open to all. Uploading information related to these fields on the social networking sites can be a threat to the internal security.

Revolution – Some countries in the world feel threatened by the fact that social media can bring the people together and thus, create a revolution. This in turn can cause political instability.

Social Networking Sites: Examples of Banning

The Social Networking Sites are banned in few counties, either wholly or partially. It is simply a kind of censorship which is taking place around the globe.

North Korea – The networking sites are blocked in this country since the advent of Internet in order to prevent the access to any communication which has not been provided by the government.

Iran – The social networking sites are blocked in Iran since 2009 after the Presidential elections. After the election of Iranian President Hasan Rouhani, the social media has played an important role in his administration's media scheme.

China – China is the most common country known for banning the social media. After the protests by Uighurs (Muslim ethnic minority of China) turned into the deadly riots, the social media started to see its extinction in the country.

Pakistan – It has blocked the YouTube since 2002, when the trailer of a controversial film appeared on the site. The name of the film was "The innocence of Muslims".

Turkey – Twitter was banned in Turkey for two weeks in 2014 and You Tube is banned since March 2014. These sites were banned to decrease the portrayal of government corruption. There were certain evidences related to the corruption of government after the 2014 election.

However, the question is if its impact has been constructive or destructive to any country. Through the course of the research we have seen how social media has been used constructively by two nations to start a dialogue and to strengthen ties, it has been used by security forces to improve security ties and spread information about hazards. It had also been used by the common man to gather strength and raise their voice for and against the government if required. However, apart from these qualities of goodness, social media also has some negative impact on national security. Like leakage of crucial information or state secrets and usage of social media by non-state actors and organizations for recruitment of radicals and spreading terrorism. It has emerged as a threat to internal security in India because of its viral posts which can impact any situation by making a region volatile and sparking tension in the area. A small tweet or one WhatsApp forward can entirely inflate a situation and cause a law and order problem.

However, we need to note that social media is still a young tool. It is still growing and in its nascent stage and rules for it are still being developed or constructed. We have to still harness the full potential of social media and how it can be used by the government for better good. Examples of the start of this revolution can be the use of social media by the government over the last few years and its effort to reach the common man. Apart from being potential threat tools, social media can represent an effective opportunity to preserve national security and/or reach the strategic interests of a state if used properly by civil institutions and, in particular, by security services and/or information security services. A continuous and deep monitoring of these media can be carried out as a warning tool in case of present and future threats to national security, since the use of social media by criminal organizations, terrorist groups, adversary states and other competitors is more and more increasing. For this reason a continuous analysis of social media by Intelligence can serve as: early warning: monitoring social media in order to recognize the first signs of an hostile or potentially dangerous activity for a state's security i.e. collecting and analyzing messages by opposing movements sent via social network sites for the organization of a violent protest can be useful in order to forestall a rebellion or to mitigate its negative consequences; studying the information shared by crackers in specialized the blogs in order to launch an information attack to a critical infrastructure can concur in adopting suitable protection counter-measures; tracking teaching videos for military recruitment, spread via YouTube by an al-Qaedist group can help find the users who make use of them, understand the attack methods and techniques and devise effective methods to react and counter the terrorist threat; the continuous control of a Facebook profile updates and a careful exam of the photos published on that very profile can allow to trace the movements and the activities of the members of a criminal group and mapping their connections, etc. It can also act as a strategic warning and horizon scanning aimed at outlining the long-and medium-term trend of threats, at identifying the orientation of the opposing groups and forecasting their choices i.e. collecting signs of protest from young people through the monitoring of the principal social networking sites can help forecast and maybe nip in the bud a dissent which could change into an organized protest movement or even in a revolutionary group; analyzing the discussions on blogs specialized in international politics and strategic studies (often held by the leading experts or by the representatives of the major think tanks) can be useful to understand the possible long-term evolutions of foreign policy and of the strategic thinking of a state's leadership; studying the discussions of blogs specialized in science and technology can help measure the possible long-term development of scientific and technological expertise in a certain place; mapping the relational networks developed on social media by members of subversive groups and analysing their evolution can allow to forecast the possible development of the group itself, etc. Using social media to obtain and analyses data for info-prevision and tactic-strategic warning purposes is of great interest to the US DoD, too, which is developing a specific program called "Social Media in Strategic Communication" (SMISC) through DARPA, with the aim of monitoring such media so as to obtain a better knowledge of the environment some units deployed abroad work into, and collect useful information to support military missions. Therefore, using social media this way can help the commanders of the

US deployed locations to better understand the socio-politic, religious, economic and cultural characteristics of the area they work in and detect emerging threats. Even in our country, Broadcast Engineering Consultants India Limited, a Government of India enterprise under the Ministry of Information and Broadcasting has invited bids for controlling the 'Social Media Communication Hub'.

Social Media and its Impact on Foreign Relations

Modi's unorthodox engagement tactics through social media platforms has also made international headlines. His use of the Weibo platform before visiting China in 2015, drew widespread attention, evident from his first post on Weibo – 'Hello China! Looking forward to interacting with Chinese friends through Weibo' being heavily forwarded and commented upon by Weibo users. His tweet on the eve of his arrival in Japan also elicited similar enthusiastic response. These messages could have been part of the push for his Act East policy targeting the region. But they also exposed the other side of social media-enabled direct communication where people are hardly restricted in voicing opinions of leaders, countries and societies. Chinese micro bloggers took the opportunity to draw Modi's attention to the plight of Indian women with one Chinese netizen posting: 'I suggest improving the social status of Indian women and protecting the safety of females! Or we foreign women will not dare travel to India'; the post, while attracting considerable attention underlined challenges that social-media active leaders like Modi can hardly avoid in their attempt to influence perceptions through digital diplomacy. The example underscores an interesting aspect of interaction through social media on image-building: *the risk of pushing particular agendas for specific purposes turning counterproductive*. In this regard, it is not clear to what extent Modi's FB and Twitter posts on his foreign visits and other achievements have actually achieved in terms of better 'perception' of India. While scholars argue 'Prime Minister Modi's charismatic interaction with world leaders' now represent 'a strategic advantage in the soft power for India in the region', India's absence from *The Soft Power 30*, an index ranking 30 countries in terms of soft power resources, underlines 'India evidently does not yet benefit as much from international awareness, positive associations, or investments in cultural diplomacy as many other countries. Unorthodox engagement tactics by Modi also include 'selfie' diplomacy that has become an integral part of his overseas travels. Again, much like his FB and Twitter posts, while breaking perception stereotypes and casting the Prime Minister in a charming and engaging light, it is not clear how selfie diplomacy has changed perceptions about India as a nation. It's interesting to note the contrasts between perceptions of Modi and India in this regard: *The Soft Power 30* report marks India's best performing area in the Digital sub-index and highlights the 'Indian Prime Minister Modi's unrivalled skills in digital diplomacy' (*The Soft Power 30* 2018).

The recognition of Modi as a champion of digital diplomacy and India's capacities as a digital nation, is in sharp contrast to its absence from the list of most successful soft power nations in the world. Communication aimed at building of *Brand Modi* and *Brand India* is aimed at the diaspora as one of its major target groups. Modi's Tweets like: 'Our diaspora are our "Rashtradoots". We are immensely proud of their accomplishments and their passion towards India & India's progress' in 2017 underscore the priority. Engaging the diaspora has been a sustained part of Modi's foreign policy communication on the firm belief that 'well-structured diaspora bonds would directly finance key development priorities. And that would give everyone in the diaspora, not just its entrepreneurs and its financiers, the opportunity to translate their long-distance patriotism into tangible economic gain and share in India's growth story, as Modi often encourages them to do'. Initiatives like e-visas and MADAD meaning 'help' for addressing grievances of the overseas Indians online are specific to the diasporas.

In this regard, however, styles of engagement between leaders have shown contrasts. Sushama Swaraj, the Foreign Minister, has been visibly dialogue-oriented in engagement: her immediate response to a tweet plea by a Yemeni woman with an 8-month old son married to an Indian in April 2015 is perhaps the best example of digital diplomacy shifting from monologue to dialogue. The *Foreign Policy* magazine acclaimed the Minister 'for fashioning a novel brand of Twitter diplomacy' and included her in the list of 100 Global Thinkers. Swaraj's social media engagement certainly appears more interactive and distinct from Modi's.

This could, however, be due to the nature of her portfolio given that the foreign ministry has to focus on addressing grievances as part of its responsibilities, which several other Ministries and Ministers, including the Prime Minister need not. In conclusion our findings have been very clear, with over 2 billion users on Facebook, 328 million on Twitter and many other platforms, the influence of social media cannot be denied. Social media is in fact used by the public to put across their views to the government nowadays and the government also listens to them through the media. The study of social media and its uses at various levels is invaluable for political activism. It can help diffuse ideas and information easily across the globe. In our survey, we found that the tool which is mostly used on social media to influence foreign policy is Twitter and Facebook, wherein the Ministry of External Affairs has also increased its activity by 400 per cent.

The PM's visit to foreign nations is covered extensively on these mediums as they are the only source of factual and correct information about the meetings between the world leaders. The spokespersons account is the constant source of news and updates for the people of the country. Social media, hence, does have the power to influence policy decisions and sway the government opinion. However, through our survey we have found that the influence is contingent on certain conditions. As there are various challenges on foreign policy reporting like lack of understanding of subject by the reporter, disclosure of information by the ministry, etc. Through our survey we found that 29 per cent users use social media for their personal use while 28 per cent use it as students. YouTube was found to be the most used with 34 per cent saying yes to our survey and then came in Facebook with 31 per cent users. Also, around 34 per cent of our respondents used social media to obtain knowledge and information, which is a big win for national security of our country. Among others, 23 per cent used for personal work, 17 per cent for upkeep of information and knowledge and 15 per cent for personal study. In fact through our survey, we found that 11 per cent or 112 respondents used social media because they were interested in foreign policy news. Through our survey, it also became clear that at least 82 respondents or 16.97 per cent users used social media to express their views on foreign policy. In fact, 22 respondents visited the official MEA website daily, 52 users visited the site monthly and 137 people visited the website occasionally to get information about foreign policies and its updates. Another important conclusion which was drawn after our survey was that at least 55 per cent or 266 respondents felt that social media incidents can change or affect policies of the government. In fact 68 per cent users said they have witnessed slight changes in policies of the government after a social media incident and 3 per cent said they witnessed complete change in the policy. The respondents even gave examples to support their claim which has been mentioned in our findings. This goes on to show how much impact social media has on people and how people perceive social media as a game changer in policy making. In our survey, 379 respondents or 78 per cent people said that social media is very important for foreign policy making. At least 59 per cent said that social media also has positive impact on national security of the country. We can draw a conclusion that people in India also think that social media is playing a greater role in policy making like in the P5 or world's top five countries. In our survey, 294 respondents or 61 per cent people said that P5 countries use social media for their governments benefit and even in India our respondents agreed that the government uses social media for policy making. 45 per cent of our respondents said that social media influences foreign policy directly. To gauge the interest of the respondents on social media and foreign policy, we concluded that 25 per cent people used social media daily to update themselves only about foreign policies on social media while 43 per cent updated themselves occasionally on social media if they wanted to know about foreign policy. We conclude from the results of our research and survey that people use social media as a tool which has an immense impact on policy making. People believe that social media is a powerful tool which can influence foreign policies and also make the government change its policies.

Recommendations

In Indian situation, we do not have fully control over the use of social media applications by the people of India because our country is democratic country. Few recommendations are made here based on the information collected from the stakeholders. The details of the recommendations are discussed in detail in the conclusion to avoid duplications.

1. A continuous and deep monitoring of these social media applications can be carried out as a warning tool in case of present and future threats to national security, since these tools are used by criminal organizations, terrorist groups and adversary states and other competitors is more and more in use and increasing rigorously.
2. Continuous analysis of social media information by Intelligence can serve as early warning for state and central government authorities. Hence it is recommended to develop such mechanism to analyses each information which is upload on social media.
3. It is recommended that **Social Media Hub** may be created to each state in India with filtration of all messages of all social media technological tools, such as WhatsApp, YouTube, Tweeter, Instagram etc. The mechanism should be developed and monitored by independent agency. And this agency should made report to State government to their respective state if anything happened wrong related to the security aspect of the state and particularly country, it should be immediately reported to Central Government to take immediate action.
4. It is also recommended to the Central Government of India to develop a tool and mechanism to identify fake news which appears in social media applications and tools and other media. Majority of the fake videos are uploaded by public or unknown persons who has created fake account on YouTube which is most powerful and preferred social media tools by public.
5. By using social media to obtain data and analyse information for info-prevision and tactic-strategic warning purposes is a great help and interest to the US DoD to develop a specific program called "Social Media in Strategic Communication (SMISC) through DARPA with the aim of monitoring such media to obtain better knowledge of the situation and environment, some units deployed abroad to work into and collect information to support missions of the Military. On the basis of this Indian government also establish such program "India SMISC" (Indian Social Media Strategic Communication).

6. It is suggested that mechanism should be develop to keep track and check on happenings abroad. This will help to our intelligence agencies to keep track on such incidents happens abroad and which are related to our country's security.
7. It is also recommended that a separate agency is to be established to collect information and public opinions on India's foreign policy from social media and provide such information to Policy makers of the Indian government which helps to frame foreign policy of India.

NOTES

1 Sharma, Loveleena: social media as A Challenge to Traditional Indian Diplomacy A Medium of Communication or A Mode of Diplomacy? Accessed through on http://www.jgu.edu.in/JJIA/PDF/vol4/Loveleena-Sharma.pdf , 2 July 2017

REFERENCES

1. Abraham, Rhea. Media and National Security. KW Publication Pvt. Ltd, New Delhi, 2011.
2. Adan, A.M. (2017), Influence of the media on foreign policy of a state: Kenya and Britain, United States International University. Thesis Report, Degree of Master of Arts (International Relations) United States International Univerisity-Africa, (2017)
3. Adan, A.M. (2017), *Influence of the media on foreign policy of a state: Kenya and Britain.* United States International University.
4. Aday, S. (2017), *The US Media, Foreign Policy, and Public Support for War.* The Oxford Handbook of Political Communication.
5. Aday, S. (2017), The US Media, Foreign Policy, and Public Support for War. The Oxford Handbook of Political Communication.
6. Allmer, Thomas. Critcal Theory and social media,Between Emancipation and Commodification. Taylor & Francis: Print Publication Date: April,2015: Online Publication Date: 2015.
7. Areg Galstyan, S.M. (2017), *Inside Russia's New Foreign Policy Master Plan.* National Interest.org.
8. Barnett, S. (2016), The tragic downfall of the British media. Foreign Policy.com, July 8, 2016, Blog, https://foreignpolicy.com/2016/07/08/the-tragic-downfall-of-british-media-tabloids-brexit
9. Barnett, S. (2016), *The tragic downfall of the British media.* Foreign Policy.com.
10. Barton, William P. (1950), "Indian Foreign Policy," *The Australian Quarterly*, Vol. 22, No. 4 (Dec., 1950), pp. 25-34, published by Australian Institute of Policy and Science Stable URL: http://www.jstor.org/stable/20633300.
11. Baru, Sanjaya (2009), "The Influence of Business and Media on Indian Foreign Policy, India Review, vol. 8, no. 3, July–September, 2009, pp. 266–285.
12. Belkin, P. (2011). France: Factors Shaping Foreign Policy, and Issues in US-French Relations. *Congressional Research Service.*

13. Bindra, Sukhwant S. (2004), "Domestic milieu of India and foreign policy making process: a theoretical perspective," *The Indian Journal of Political Science*, Vol. LXV, No. 2, April-June, 2004.
14. Khare V. S. 'B.R. Ambedkar and India's National Security' Kilaso Press New Delhi 2005.
15. Khare V.S. 'Terrorism and Counter Terrorism' Pentagon Press, New Delhi 2019.
16. Khare V.S. (2020), *Influence of Social Media on India's Foreign Policy Making*, New Delhi: Pentagon Press LLP. ISBN 978-93-90095-20-9.
17. Khare V.S. (2020), *Politics of Climate Change & Global Peace and Security*, New Delhi: Pentagon Press LLP. ISBN 978-93-90095-21-6.
18. Khare V.S. (2020), *General BC Joshi Memorial Lectures on National Security*, New Delhi: Pentagon Press LLP. ISBN 978-93-90095-23-0.

2

Impact of Social Media on Peace and Security

Dr. Anna Opalka

University of Applied Sciences in Nysa

University of Applied Sciences in Nysa was founded in 2001 as a public university that provides education on the 14 fields of study: Technical (Computer Science, Production management, Architecture, Economical (Finance and Banking), Sociological (Internal Security), Medical (Nursing, Medical rescue, Public Health, Cosmetology, Dietetics, Philological: English, German, Business English), Art (Jazz and Pop Music). The university has already promoted 10,000 graduates and provides education for about 4500 students. The University of Applied Sciences in Nysa is rapidly developing. The laboratory equipment conforms to the highest European standards as well as plays a significant role in research activities. There are two R&D Centres within the university's structure: R&D Centre for Conservation and Renovation and Regional Centre for Knowledge Transfer and Innovative Technology in Nysa. Research and Development Centre for Renovation and Conservation together with Institute of Architecture will play a crucial role in the project. Institution will build the Box Kit regarding the cultural heritage protection that has been the main research area of mentioned units in recent years. The Centre is an institution established to protect cultural heritage and to coordinate all actions in the preservation of monuments. The main scope of the activity is to conduct art conservation research into the composition and identification of painting layers, mortars, supports, stone, wood as well as into the structure analysis—stratigraphy, construction, inventory of historical objects; it also carries out the analysis of materials and art conservation technologies, conservation and restoration of movable and architectural monuments, supervision over renovation works, photographic, drawing and descriptive documentation. Regional Centre for Knowledge Transfer and Innovative Technology in Nysa is a bridge connecting the market expectations with entrepreneurs' experience and the University of Applied Sciences in Nysa academic teachers' knowledge. Thanks to the staff's achievements, their passion and acquaintance of the current market needs, the Centre offers professional assistance, expert advice as well as complex business services addressed to: entrepreneurs, public administration workers, local governments, graduates, researchers as well as to any other institutions from the Opole Province and the whole country. This Centre will play an important role in the dissemination and realization of project's results. Thus the main University's mission is education for professional market also international cooperation and research are one of the most important elements of the strategic development plan of our institution. From the beginning of it existence The University of Applied Sciences in Nysa has established contacts with partners abroad and has a great experience in applying and managing educational and research projects at international level, including Erasmus, Leonardo da Vinci, Comenius, Culture 2000, Phare CBC and Interreg as well as research projects founded by national public funds. The University is strongly connected with regional schools organizing the Nysa Science Festivals variety of projects connected.

Research and Development Centre for Conservation and Renovation of UAS in Nysa

- Conservation and research laboratories of the R&D Centre: analytical laboratory, chemical laboratory, aging laboratory, art restoration laboratory.
- Newest specialist devices such as Rafaello and Smart Clean Lasers,

JSM-630LA scanning microscope with EDS analyser, a holding chamber, a climatic chamber and many others.

Within the **Institute of Technical Sciences/Computer Sciences Faculty** the following laboratories are operating at the moment: computer games and multimedia laboratory, CISCO computer networks laboratory, computer graphics and design laboratory, electronic laboratory, computer architecture laboratory, virtual systems laboratory, fiber networks laboratory, management systems supporting laboratory for AutoCAD, CAD/CAE, Mechanical Desktop, Inventor, KSPT, MTS, MS Project, CDN XL.

Regional Innovative Centre for Technology Transfer carries out research activity, consultancy and transfer of technology to construction industry and is equipped with:

- Laboratory of 3DScannng.
- Laboratory of Drone's implementation into the didactic process.
- Fully equipped classrooms, workshop sites and conference rooms.
- Pre-incubation area for graduates and SMEs co-operatives.

Communication: Definitions and Functions

Since ages communication channels between people are confronted with various kinds of risks, among which we may name information disruptions, loss of initial meaning, lack of security or many others. To understand the genesis of that fact we need to look into the definitions of the communication system itself. The main components of the communication process are the following:

- *Context:* every communication is affected by the context in which it takes place. This context may be physical, social, chronological or cultural.
- *Sender/encoder:* it is a person who sends the message by usage of symbols (words or graphic or visual aids, gestures) to convey the message and to produce the required response.
- *Message:* a key idea that the sender wants to communicate. It must be ensured that the main objective of the message is clear.

- *Encoding* (Communication symbol): the process of any communication subject matter conversion, which is always abstract and intangible. Transmission of message requires use of certain symbols.
- *Medium:* it is a means used to exchange/transmit the message.
- *Recipient/Decoder:* it is a person for whom the message is intended/aimed/targeted. The degree to which the decoder understands the message is dependent upon various factors such as knowledge of recipient, their responsiveness to the message and the reliance of encoder on decoder. Decoding: the process of translation of an encoded message into ordinary understandable language. Receiver converts the symbols, words or signs receiver from the sender to get the meaning of the message.
- *Feedback:* the main component of communication process as it permits the sender to analyse the efficiency of the message. It helps the sender in confirming the correct interpretation of message by the decoder. Feedback may be verbal or non-verbal and in social media it became a list of shortcuts, like emoticons and graphic symbols or short commends.

In simple words, communication is the sending of a message from a source to a receiver with the least possible loss of meaning. The process of communication happens when speaker sends a message that is in some kind of code. The listener decodes the message and responds, thereby giving the speaker feedback. If any kind of disturbance blocks any step of communication, the message will be destroyed or manipulated and it will bring a chaos to the initial meaning. Let's not forget about the upper layers that stand behind the information so difficult to understand while communication occurs via internet tools with not having the immediate feedback (physical layer) from the receiver that could clarify the meaning of the message. In fact social media leaves the space for self-decoding the information which disrupts its natural intention.

Figure 1: Communication flow and effective communication disruptors.

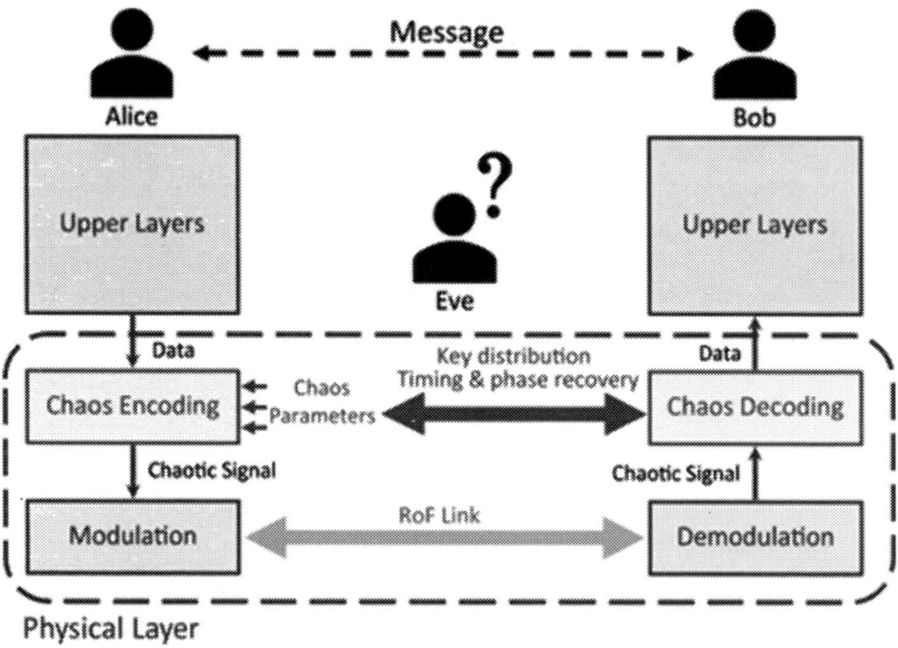

Some disturbances in the communication process may come from:

1. Perceptual, cultural and language differences
2. Information overload
3. Inattention
4. Time pressures
5. Distraction/noise
6. Emotions
7. Complexity in organizational structure
8. Poor retention

One of the most important disturbances comes from cultural differences in perception and communication. Along with the definitions culture is a shared system of meanings, beliefs, values behaviours through which experience is interpreted and carried out. That's why culture is the "lens" through which you view the world, it's central to what you see, how you make sense of what you see or how you express yourself. There are many factors that create an individual or a group culture such as beliefs, language, customs, rituals, behaviours, religions, food, art, attitudes among others. It's almost impossible to standardize the information in a way that it will be identical in meaning to everyone in the globe. It's only a question of how much it is modified and how to help people to understand each other. For a well-educated person in that matter it is easy to use that knowledge in order to influence others or to create communication flow according to personal objectives.

At the same time every organization that influences others opinions is aware how strong importance lies in the selection of the communication streams, tools and strategies. The communication process is a source of information, creates points of view and attitudes, helps in socializing as well as building directed motivation and what's more it is a powerful controlling tool.

Social Media: Phenomenon and Statistics

Kaplan and Heanlein (2010) have characterized social media as gathering of internet construct applications that work with respect to the ideological and technological establishments of the internet and that permit the creation and exchange of user-generated content. Thanks to the rapid information systems development political communication is assisted worldwide by social media through the exchange of information, the exposure of wrongdoing by elites, and mobilization and coordination of different ideological protests. Connections between activists are made easier; coordination and communication are less costly than ever. But more than ever in history the flow once launched in social media is practically 2018, unstoppable and brings strong consequences for longer periods. Moreover, potential allies and activists can be targeted and recruited in the context of political violence and radicalization (ISIS example).

In the recent years social media has grown from innocent time consuming hobby to a global opinion influencer. Facebook estimated that 2.7 billion people use Facebook, WhatsApp, Instagram, or Messenger each month and more than 2 billion people use at least one of the Facebook family of services every day on an average (53 million users of social media only in the US).Internet has become the world's biggest trash of information (teens spend up to 9 hours a day on social platforms which is actually more then we interact with family and friends).[1]

1. Worldwide, there are over 2.32 billion monthly active users (MAU) as of December 31, 2018. This is a 9 percent increase in Facebook MAUs year over year. This is compared to 2.27 billion MAUs for Q3 2018. (Source: Facebook 1/30/19) Facebook is simply too big to ignore as a digital marketing communications programme.
2. There are 1.15 billion mobile daily active users (Mobile DAU) for December 2016, an increase of 23 percent year over year (Source: Facebook as of 2/01/17). This is hugely significant and shows the dramatic growth of mobile traffic on Facebook. Please note that this was the last official division received in IR press releases of a delineation of mobile DAU from other metrics. Mobile advertising revenue is reported according to Facebook to represent approximately 93 percent of advertising revenue for Q4 2018 up from 89 percent in Q4 2017.
3. 1.52 billion people on average log onto Facebook daily and are considered daily active users (Facebook DAU) for December 2018. This represents a 9 percent increase year over year (Source: Facebook as 1/30/19). Sixty-six percent of Facebook's audience would be considered DAU versus Monthly Active Users (MAU). The Implication: A huge and vastly growing number of Facebook users are active and consistent in their visits to the site, making them a promising audience for your marketing efforts. Growth was experienced across all global regions for the fourth quarter of 2018.
4. There are 1.74 billion mobile active users (Mobile Facebook MAU) for December 2016 which is an increase of 21 per cent year-over-year (Source: Facebook as of 02/01/17).
5. On an average, the Like and Share Buttons are viewed across almost 10 million websites daily. (*Source: Facebook* as of 10/2/2014)
6. In Europe, over 307 million people are on Facebook. (*Source: Search Engine Journal*) The Takeaway: This isn't just a US phenomenon – a worldwide market is available via Facebook.
7. Age 25 to 34, at 29.7 per cent of users, is the most common age

demographic (*Source: E marketer* 2012). What this means for you: This is also the prime target demographic for the marketing of many businesses, and is gives a chance to engage these key consumers on Facebook.

8. Five new profiles are created every second. (*Source: ALL Facebook* 2012). The Implication: potential audience on Facebook is growing exponentially for businesses.
9. Facebook users are 76 per cent female (out of 100 per cent of all females) and 66 per cent male (out of 100 per cent of all males).This state is one that you really have to think about because it's comparing the percentage of all females against the percentage of all males who are on Facebook. To dig a little deeper take a look at this study which does a much better job at explaining the nuances (*Source: Brand watch* – https://www.brandwatch.com/2015/01/men-vs-women-active-social-media/). The Takeaway: Since this isn't a large statistical difference, you should be able to effectively reach both genders on Facebook.
10. Highest traffic occurs mid-week between 1 to 3 pm. (*Source: Bit.ly blog*) On another note, a Facebook post at 7pm will result in more clicks on an average than posting at 8pm (*Source: Forbes*). How this can help you: You have the potential to reach more consumers and drive higher traffic to your site during peak usage times, but people may be more likely to be more engaged in the evenings. This statistic may be a factor when you are planning social communication scheduling. (Also consider that Facebook has a global audience, so you may want to plan around the time zone of your key market.)
11. On Thursdays and Fridays, engagement is 18 per cent higher (*Source: Bit.ly blog*). The Implication: Again, use this information to determine when to post in order to optimize your social media marketing efforts.
12. There are 83 million fake profiles (*Source: CNN*). The Takeaway: Nothing is perfect, so always remain thoughtful and strategic in your efforts. Also, fake or not, these are still potential consumers. There are various reasons for fake profiles, including

professionals doing testing and research, and people who want to segment their Facebook use more than is possible with one account.

13. Photo uploads total 300 million per day (*Source: Gizmodo*). The Implication: Again, this is an indication of engaged users; also, it is an indication that there are a lot of photos, as well as other information, competing for users' attention, so target your efforts strategically.
14. Average time spent per Facebook visit is 20 minutes (*Source: Infodocket*). What this means for you: You could have a short time period to make your impression, so use it wisely with relevant, interesting and unique posts and offers in order to get the most return on your efforts.
15. Every 60 seconds on Facebook: 510,000 comments are posted, 293,000 statuses are updated, and 136,000 photos are uploaded (*Source: The Social Skinny*). The Implication: Again, there are a lot of engaged and active users, but also a huge amount of information competing for their attention, so quality and strategy on your part matter.
16. 4.75 billion pieces of content shared daily as of May 2013 which is a 94 percent increase from August 2012 (*Source: Facebook*).
17. Fifty per cent of 18-24 year-olds go on Facebook when they wake up (*Source: The Social Skinny*). What this means for you: Facebook is important to these users, and potentially, if done correctly, so is the content you post on it.
18. One in five page views in the United States occurs on Facebook (*Source: Infodocket* 2012). How this helps you: This is a huge market on the web; if you use social media marketing efforts on Facebook well, you could have huge returns to show for it.
19. Forty-two per cent of marketers report that Facebook is critical or important to their business (*Source: State of Inbound Marketing* 2012). The Takeaway: This is a crowded marketplace, but you can't afford to sit it out, because odds are fairly high that your competition is there. The key is to use Facebook marketing correctly and make sure that your efforts stand out from the crowd.

20. Sixteen million local business pages have been created as of May 2013 which is a 100 percent increase from 8 million in June 2012 (*Source: Facebook*). Facebook marketing has transformed how business is conducted, and its use by local businesses to extend their markets continues to explode.

This phenomenon of social media is a fusion of sociology and technology, transforming monologues (one to many) into dialogues (many to many) and is the democratization of information, transforming people from content readers into authors. What's more, in all that process you may stay anonymous to some extend that encourages users to act more and more freely and with no limitations for content and presentation. But according to the psychological researches permanent using the social media causes some tremendous psychological changes in people's behaviour and decision-making process 2018, and some of them are as follows:

1. Losing the gap between real life and social media;
2. Fear of "missing out" leading to depression and anxiety;
3. Letting our gadgets to consume our time pretty pointlessly;
4. Social media users are an easy target for online ads (children as the most vulnerable 45 per cent children admitted that they experienced cyber bullying).

After accepting social media as a powerful communication tool it is not surprising that leaders and governments are heavily active on social media to campaign, to gather support for their issues at home and abroad, and to influence and/or bypass traditional media in a way to achieve the certain goals of the organisation. Nowadays social media are a kind of chaotic and dynamic system that (from the mathematic point of view) is very sensitive to initial conditions, is topologically mixing, its periodic orbits are dense enough to confuse the receivers and to manipulate facts and opinions worldwide. But in this, chaos might be a method that could influence the young generations in a positive way while there is no escape from them anyway. Let's mention at least some opportunities in using the social media in a reasonable and constructive way.

1. It is the greatest tool for expression and sharing of information (utilizing them is another issue and depends on its user's intention).

2. It is a platform for exchanging democratic dialogue, conflict prevention and peace building among cultures and generations.
3. It is a tool in creating peace by taking conflict resolution and strategies to a social network platform, leading to peace-building intercultural dialogues among members of the social setup, and coming up with theories with regard to the same.
4. Warning and alerts tool for conflicts in order to take precaution.

From the other hand there are many threats and risks that could totally disrupt the above mentioned opportunities and to make the whole process pointless, for instance:

- Troubles of ensuring reliability and accountability of facts and information disseminated through Internet.
- Troubles regarding the precision of the information contextualization or authentication of such information.
- Social media act in unpredictable ways and without regulations, ethical standards or professionalism any individual posting material can make events and revise them, there is also a huge de-formalization of communication.
- It has decreased face-to-face interactions, there have been issues of reliability of information presented, concentration, ownership of media content, and the meaning of interactions created by social media.
- Social media can also lead to destabilization of peace

Social Media in Business and Education

The growth of social media is already having a tremendous impact on business throughout the world, because social media is changing the rules of the marketplace, just like the Internet did a decade ago and no one—not even the experts know what the total impact it will have on the marketplace. But it is clear that times are changing again, and those that do not embrace social media will go the way of print media. Companies now a days have more insight into the consumer perception of their products and services than ever before what influences the adequate products development according to consumer needs. Having no longer complete control of their products and services perception by the consumers they have to participate in an online marketing game of contemporary times. Although social media is a collective action, in reality, it is the result of millions of individual monologues and dialogues. Listening to, learning from, measuring and engaging in the millions of consumer conversations in social media are now the keys to success for companies in their marketing efforts. Companies that engage with consumers will find that they have ability to guide their brand; the companies that ignore customer communications within social media will find their brand disconnected from their buyers. Business success in the coming years will require companies to value the power of social conversations to connect and collaborate in real-time communities.

Universities worldwide also cannot ignore social media and use them in order to communicate and create information directed to various stakeholders, like students, graduates, parents, staff members, companies, business and academic partners as well as authorities and society. One of the main objectives of the Universities nowadays is to inform students how to protect themselves from negative information impact and manipulation. Since the young generation is the most vulnerable because of its psychological, social and physiological immaturity, it needs protection from harmful information impact, which is spread through the Internet. In this regard, educators need to undertake important challenges for implementing them to the study programmes. Some of the preliminary content towards social media education should include the following:

- to identify the level of the participants' competences in a matters of information security;
- to provide methodological assistance to young people on issues of information security;
- to show the algorithm of user's actions to ensure information security;
- to create conditions for young people in understanding of their own Internet culture;
- to attract young people's attention to the problem of the competent use of the internet resources;

- to acquaint participants with the laws that ensure information security; and
- to create a responsible attitude and awareness towards the importance of safe behaviour in the network.

Universities have been seen as communities dedicated to the learning and personal development of their members, especially students ('liberal' theory) and sources of expertise and vocational identity (the 'professional formation' theory). They are also perceived as creators, testers, and sites for the evaluation and application of new knowledge (the 'research engine' theory, with an important corollary—the 'business and industry services' theory) and important contributors to society and nations (the 'civic and community engagement' theory)[2]. But the most important mission of modern educational institution is the obligation to offer rational and timely criticism in areas of public policy and social and economic life and to teach individuals critical and independent thinking. Having this in mind University Communication strategy towards social media should be connected to Mission of the University, Strategy development as well as University language policy. It requires:

- defining objectives
- defining success factors and indicators
- building roadmap (with a time horizon)
- usage of adequate resources

In this regard, the learning methodologies need to be more focused on more interaction between learners (workshops, projects, etc.) as well as towards soft skills then self-study. There are many other factors that should be taken into account by university's information policy makers in order to educate and secure future generations from manipulation and communication chaos. University's social media marketing policy is the process of promoting not only the offer of the institution but also the values that stand behind the academic performance. It has limitless benefits—from forging close, professional relationships, to dramatically boosting visibility, traffic, reputation and programmes offered. But even the most basic focus into social media marketing can yield tremendous results starting from identification through building relationships with the target audience towards building the tolerant and cooperative communities. To summarise the chapter, it has to be said that on educational institutions lies enormous responsibility towards preventing young generation from the risk of being manipulated by social media and luckily they may bare this bargain in the best possible way if they only modify their policies according to the contemporary challenges in youth education like social media existence.

REFERENCES

1. Core Data points Review & Updated Wednesday, January 30, 2019, based upon Facebook's official investor relations information.This information is officially updated once per quarter.
2. Watson et al (2011), pp. 1–28.

3

Information Economy the Need for High Standards of Ethics and Accountability in Social Media for a Positive Outcome

Dr. Ecaterina Daniela Zeca

Introduction

People decide what technologies and what products to develop and use, determine when a product is safe to be launched on the market and make decisions about the requirements the product has to meet. People approve laws, normative acts and standards. So that it is about us, about what we want to have, to do, to become. Us means the individual user, the company, the economic environment, the administration and the politics. Regarding Social Media in society, looking in the past, it is noted that for some time there was a restraint in the dissemination of information about the real possibilities created by this new technology. The new facilities created by it SM have been used primarily for military purposes. Any revolution in technique causes changes, with positive and negative effects.

1. Positive Effects of Internet and Social Media

The Internet has revolutionized communication on the planet. The

Internet network seems to replace what in the past meant the famous commercial roads that started from the Orient, connected the continents between them and brought much prosperity to those who controlled them. Similarly, platforms, Internet infrastructure and Big Data warehouses will give great prestige to the owners.

However, the use of Social Media remodels the society, with positive socio-economic reverberations for all mankind (Figure 1).

Figure 1: Social Media Remodels our way to be, to relate to each other, to work, to live, to learn, and to teach

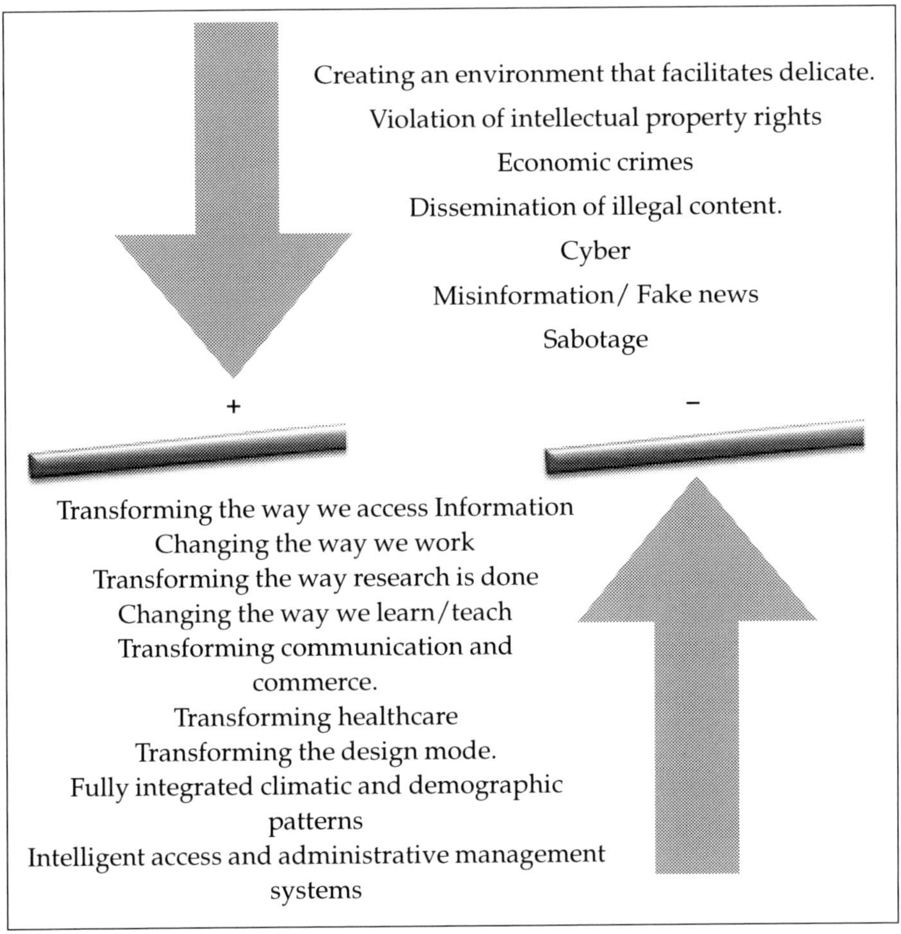

Source: De Zeca

Internet and Social Media (SM) transform the way we access information

As mentioned, information has become ubiqua, fluid, can be accessed, interrogated or imprinted whether it is: an e-book, law, magazine, recipe or audio-video information. *SM improves the way we communicate.*

The Internet network can be accessed by more than 3.27 billion people (Graph 1). Real-time virtual meetings, banking transactions have become a way to be. Simultaneously and automatically, translation is provided from multiple languages, and hardware and software allow anyone to access, regardless of physical limits.

Graph 1: Global Internet Users 2008-2015

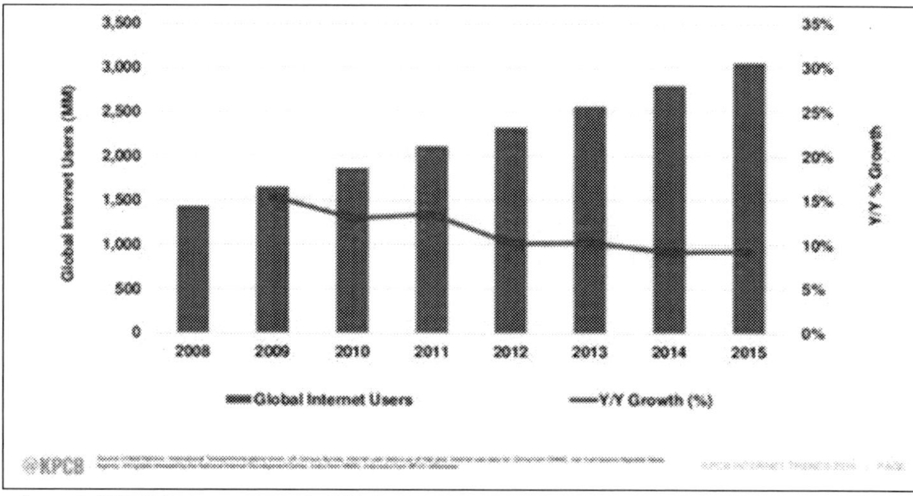

Source: KPC8 Internet trends 2016.

Internet and SM remodels the way we work

The ubiquity of information, supported by the hard and soft infrastructure, has led to the ubiquity of the workers so that a worker can access the job, no matter where he/she is (teleworking).

Such a job has great flexibility and can be adapted to the needs of every individual, from physically disabled to the elderly.

Internet and SM transforms the way research is done

Research can be done in virtual labs, on platforms regardless of their location in certain geographic coordinates. Researchers interact with each other, and access resources, change, share, access information and access digital libraries. There is scientific documentation available online, allowing access to published research.

Changing the way we learn

Everyone can participate in online educational programs, regardless of their geographical location. Educational programs can be tailored to the needs of each individual, so that the information revolution can reach everyone and that no one is outside development possibilities. For the university environment there are educational platforms, a very well known being Massive Open Online Course (MOOC).

Figure 2: Poster, Titled "MOOC, every letter is Negotiable", Exploring the Meaning of the Words "Massive Open Online Course"

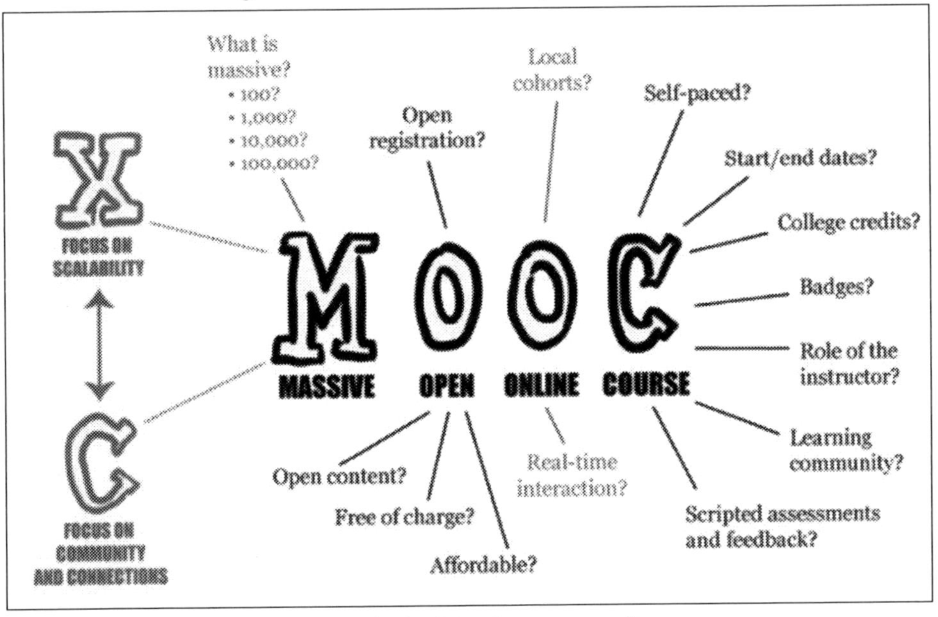

Source: https://en.wikipedia.org/wiki/Massive_open_online_course

Massive Open Online Course (MOOC) is an online course aimed at unlimited participation and open access via the web. In addition to traditional course materials such as filmed lectures, readings, and problem sets, many MOOCs provide interactive courses with user forums to support community interactions among students, professors, and teaching assistants (TAs) as well as immediate feedback to quick quizzes and assignments. MOOCs are a recent and widely researched development in distance education which were first introduced in 2006 and emerged as a popular mode of learning in 2012.

Internet and SM Transform Communication and Commerce

B2B, B2C, but also M2M communications have become current ways to do business. Any business company can easily be approached by customers, regardless of their geographic location. Companies analyze customer response with specialized software and then adjust marketing strategy, modify stock of products, etc, by using Internet and social media

Transform Healthcare

Telemedicine applications have become commonplace. Specialists use video conferencing and remote consultation methods to treat patients located a few hundred miles from a doctor. Computer-assisted surgery can be disseminated by online transmission. Physician activity is assisted by Expert Systems, based on the analysis of a large amount of medical information. "Patients can make decisions about their own treatment through new patterns of interaction with their physicians and on the basis of increasing access to biomedical information through digitized medical libraries on the Internet." Complex structures can be designed and simulated by computer. Multiple situations can be explored quickly to determine which ones are optimal, resulting (i.e. prosthesis)) in safe and high quality.

Fully Integrated Climatic and Demographic Patterns

Fully integrated climatic models allow those interested to quickly access information on "population trends, trends in climate change, resource use" for decision-making in a documented way.

Intelligent Access and Administrative Management Systems

Administration services, with the right infrastructure, can be accessed by anyone interested, on the basis of protocols, independent of their geographic location, their level of computer knowledge or their physical ability to move. Intelligent systems guide citizens by providing them with the way to get the information they are looking for. Documents and forms are accessed, filled and, subject to electronic approval, the information is processed and transmitted.

2. Negative Effects of Internet and Social Media

Violation of privacy of personal data

As personal data are used by employees for various purposes (depending on the work they are expected to do using the data), so there is a risk for customers becoming victims of "aggression informatics", which can manifest in the following forms:

Unauthorized use of data by employees whose task is to update information files.

- Accidental leakage of information through the negligence or lack of attention of some employees or through the access of intruders.
- Propagation of errors and damage caused by them.
- Deliberate use of data for purposes that some people consider to be objectionable.

Violation of intellectual property rights

Books, articles, songs, works of art, films, dramatic plays, artistic interpretations, computer programmes are protected by copyright. But, these values can be easily multiplied and diffused due to SM.

Computing programmes are copied illegally around the world every year. Multimedia programmes broadcast over the Internet have expanded the scope for infringement of intellectual property rights.

Economic Crimes

Between freedom of expression and the dissemination of illegal content: Internet messaging is completely liberalized and can be initiated by individuals or businesses without any approval, and is clearly different from those made via radio or television companies.

Cyber-Terrorism

Cyber terrorism resulted from the convergence between organized crime (profit-driven), terrorist groups (ideologically motivated) and all of it was supported by technology. It could be possible, for example, that by means of a virus (IT) invasion, the transport system, urban, regional, international, can no longer be coordinated, the water or electricity supply systems are shut down, the automated industrial processes be stopped. The European Economic and Social Committee pay special attention both to the creation of a regulatory framework regulating the Social Media field and the information security issue.

"In January 2018, the European Commission set up a high-level group of experts ("the HLEG") to advise on policy initiatives to counter fake news and disinformation spread online. The main deliverable of the HLEG was a report designed to review best practices in the light of fundamental principles, and suitable responses stemming from such principles.

The analysis presented in the Report starts from a shared understanding of disinformation as a phenomenon that goes well beyond the term. It does not cover issues arising from the creation and dissemination online of illegal content (notably defamation, hate speech, incitement to violence), which are subject to regulatory remedies under EU or national laws, nor other forms of deliberate but not misleading distortions of facts such a satire and parody.

The HLEG advises the Commission against simplistic solutions. Any form of censorship either public or private should clearly be avoided. The HLEG's recommendations aim instead to provide short-term responses to the most pressing problems, longer-term responses to increase societal resilience to disinformation, and a framework for ensuring that the effectiveness of these responses is continuously evaluated, while new evidence-based responses are developed.

The multi-dimensional approach recommended by the HLEG is based on a number of interconnected and mutually reinforcing responses. These responses rest on five pillars designed to: enhance transparency of online news, involving an adequate and privacy-compliant sharing of data about the systems that enable their circulation online; promote media and information literacy to counter disinformation and help users navigate the digital media environment; develop tools for empowering users and journalists to tackle disinformation and foster a positive engagement with fast-evolving information technologies; safeguard the diversity and sustainability of the European news media ecosystem, and promote continued research on the impact of disinformation in Europe to evaluate the measures taken by different actors and constantly adjust the necessary responses."

"The increased frequency of debate does not necessarily translate into a robust exchange of conflicting or diverse ideas. Social media 'bots' increase polarisation by manufacturing and disseminating content that reinforces skewed user beliefs. 'Bots' are easily programmable accounts on Facebook and, especially, Twitter that automatically generate content. Often, authentic account holders who receive fabricated content do not know they are interacting with'bots' (Guilbeault and Woolley). 'Bots' are in widespread use and have already demonstrated a capacity for disruption. A single 'bot' account can send out thousands of tweets a day, drowning out real Twitter users who may offer relevant, and potentially productive, dialogue on social media. Searching for content using key terms, 'bots' are designed to redistribute (e.g., retweet) this material without verifying its validity. Marginal and/or extremely partisan actors can co-opt trending discussion to give their issue areas traction especially when they program 'bots' to redistribute their content on their behalf. In recent months, social media networks have facilitated the propagation of false and disruptive stories, which users accept at face value. The danger is that fake news has already started to shake the confidence citizens have in their institutions and leaders. The proliferation of alternative, non-traditional media sites (i.e., fake news) has accelerated this in recent years. The incentive to misinform on social media networks is, in fact, profit. Dramatic and often false stories increase clicks on sites trying to attract readers. Social media networks have facilitated the propagation of false and disruptive stories, which users accept at face value. The danger is that fake news has already started to shake the confidence citizens have in their institutions and leaders. False stories can be rapidly transmitted to multiple websites, gaining traction in the news cycle before content editors at major news agencies have time to intervene and question sources".

3. Conclusion

As in prehistoric days, the use of fire transformed and reorganized society, introducing new practices, and new priorities in the communities, social media is similarly transforming the 21st century humanity as a complement, acting as a sixth sense to make us more efficient. It is very clear that social media has changed and will reshape information systems in all areas of existence, will change mentalities and will offer solutions that seemed impossible till now. The way social media is used depends on each user, but more than that, depends on education, legislation, procedures, infrastructure and motivation to use it.

Peace and Security depends on WHAT we want to get and WHERE we want to get it from. Social media is only a tool. So, ultimately the power and social effects of social media depend on human intelligence and human aspirations. What kind of problems does social media solve—networking professionally and personally, promoting social learning and knowledge sharing, marketing of a brand, communicating during a crisis/disaster, exchanging ideas, education, staying updated, etc.

Perhaps the most concerning aspect of social media is that it encourages people to share personal information. Educating yourself as to how one should use social media is very important. A comprehensive and well-defined policy should be established to prevent abuse and reduce risk while using social media.

The latest achievements in the field of information science and technology have transformed the Internet into an "agora", a place where ideas, new concepts, new technologies are designed and changed, in which contacts between all kinds of people are not only possible but become reality. Responsibility is a problem of social education. The educational process must go far beyond the doors of the school, high school or university.

This idea keeps its validity today and becomes even more important. The study of the University of Würzburg states that in order to be able to fight the crimes committed through Social Media, a relevant international strategy should be established which aims at: Improving legislation in the field of MS, Technological soft-cryptographic features that eliminate the possibility of decryption. In the educational environment, the academic field must extend the preventive concepts, being more effective than the punitive ones.

REFERENCES

1. Cordy Jane, 2017, *The Social Media Revolution: Political and Security Implications Report,* (Canada).
2. MacmillanSteup, Matthias (8 September 2017). Zalta, Edward N.,ed., *The Stanford Encyclopedia of Philosophy. Metaphysics Research Lab, Stanford University – via Stanford Encyclopedia of Philosophy.*
3. Porter, Noah, ed. (1913). *Webster's Revised Unabridged Dictionary. G& C. Merriam Co.* p. 501. Archived from the original on 15 October 2013. Retrieved 29 January 2014.
5. Vasiu Lucian, Despre importanta tehnologiilor de securitate a informatiei. Accessed at https://academiaromana.ro/pro_pri/doc/st_b03.doc on 13 February 2019.
6. Massive open online course, Accessed at https://e n.wikipedia.org/wiki/ Massive_open_online_course on 13 February 2019.
7. HLEG, 2018. Final report of the High Level Expert Group on Fake News and Online Disinformation. Accessed at https://ec.europa.eu/digital-single-market/en/ news/final-report-high level-expert-group-fake-news-and-online-disinformation on 21 January 2019.
8. The High Level Expert Group (HLEG) 2018, Final report of the High Level Expert Group on Fake News and Online Disinformation, accessed at https://ec.europa.eu/ digital-single-market/en/news/final-report-high-level-expert-group-fake-news-and-online-disinformation on 13 January 2019.
9. Committee on the Civil Dimension of Security (CDS) 2017, The Social Media Revolution: Political And Security Implications, Accessed at https://www.nato-pa.int/download-file?filename=sites/default/files/2017-09/2017%20-%20158%20CDSDG%2017%20E%20-%20SOCIAL%20MEDIA%20 REVOLUTION%20-%20CORDY%20REPORT_0.pdf on 10 January 2019.

4

Social Media Impact on Security from Internationalisation Perspective

Dr. Iryna Kramar

Social media originated as a way to interact with friends and family but later it was adopted by businesses which took advantage of it to reach out to customers. Companies use social media to find and engage with customers, drive sales through advertising and promotion, gauge consumer trends, and offering customer service or support. Nowadays even governments and politicians use social media to engage with constituents and voters.

Social media platforms offer new spaces for dialogue and allow people to listen and speak to each other in cyber space especially when they are not able to meet physically. This especially has potential in areas where personal meetings are logistically, legally and politically impossible. This can help to maintain channels of communication and is important in different areas – business, politics etc.

Social media is a useful tool in politics to be used by peace-builders to broaden a process, hearing the views of a broad range of stakeholders, without necessarily enlarging the negotiation table as such. For example, during the consultative phase of Libyan National Conference Process, HD developed an interactive website, informing Libyans about meetings and allowing them to share their views. In the Havana talks between the Colombian government and the FARC, the negotiators initiated an online consultation via a dedicated website and app. This generated thousands of written inputs from Colombian citizens about different aspects of the negotiation agendas.

Brief analysis of social media impact on peace and security in Ukraine is shown below. Statistics published by the Kiev International Institute for Sociology (KMIS) show that 72 percent of Ukrainians mainly use Ukrainian television and online media to stay informed. Only a fifth of the population regularly uses Ukrainian and Russian information sources, whereby a high level of distrust of Russian media prevails. According to the KMIS only four percent of users trust these media [1].

It is defined that television plays the main role in informing the public in Ukraine. According to a survey conducted in March 2016 in Kiev by the Gorshenin Institute, 88 percent of Ukrainians mainly use television to stay informed about current affairs; only 12.5 percent of Ukraine's citizens still read newspapers to keep up with current affairs; 29.9 percent of the population mainly uses Ukrainian news websites to stay informed.[1]

Media experts report that online media outlets have long since overtaken radio and print media as the main sources of information. Compared to other countries Internet access in Ukraine is cheap and the online products of the mass media are free.

All citizens have free access to online media. In this context a key role is played by a few opinion-makers who cleverly exploit the social media to their own advantage and have achieved a level of popularity attained only by rock stars or actors elsewhere. These individuals are political activists, journalists or politicians, whereby the dividing lines between these professions have become blurred. Their publications, be they in the form of a blog or posts on Facebook, are often more influential and reach a larger audience than any Ukrainian newspaper.

Russia's "hybrid war" in the east of the country and the accompanying mass propaganda against Ukraine provoked the desire in Kiev's government circles to adopt countermeasures that still influence the country's media policy today. The measures also highlighted how willing certain sections of the political elite in Kiev are to rashly place restrictions on media freedom in Ukraine. In August 2014 the Ukrainian government banned 15 Russian TV channels from broadcasting in Ukraine.

It is also important to understand that depending on mentality, different social media are mostly used in the country. The most popular social media websites in the world as of January 2019 are defined as follows:[2]

1. Facebook (2.27 billion users as of January 2019)
2. YouTube (1.9 B).
3. WhatsApp (1.5 B).
4. Facebook Messenger (1.3 B).
5. WeChat (1.08 B).
6. Instagram (1 B).
7. QQ (803 M).
8. QZone (531 M).
9. Douyin/Tik Tok (500 M).
10. Sino Weibo (446 M).

But for example, In Kiev and western Ukraine Facebook has more users than in other regions. At the same time Twitter is used mainly by journalists and politicians. Ukrainians don't use Twitter much because they like to express their opinion and Twitter is brief to do that and more news-oriented.

Another important aspect to be analysed in the paper is attention to social media users, in particular to define the main age group of people who mostly use social media to better use social media opportunities.

It was found out that youth, Generation D, is the one who are most active social media users. Generation D (Digital - Millennials) implies an attitude and mind of those who totally enjoy and are comfortable with the advances of the high tech world.

On the Figure 1 it is shown the proportion of youth VS total population using Internet.

The successors to the New Millennials, Generation Ds are the first true 'digital natives'. Born between 1994 and 2002, Generation Ds cannot remember a world without the internet. Academic Mark Prensky defines them as those for whom the use of technology is an inherent, not a learned, part of life.

Figure 1: Youth VS Total Population Using Internet[3]

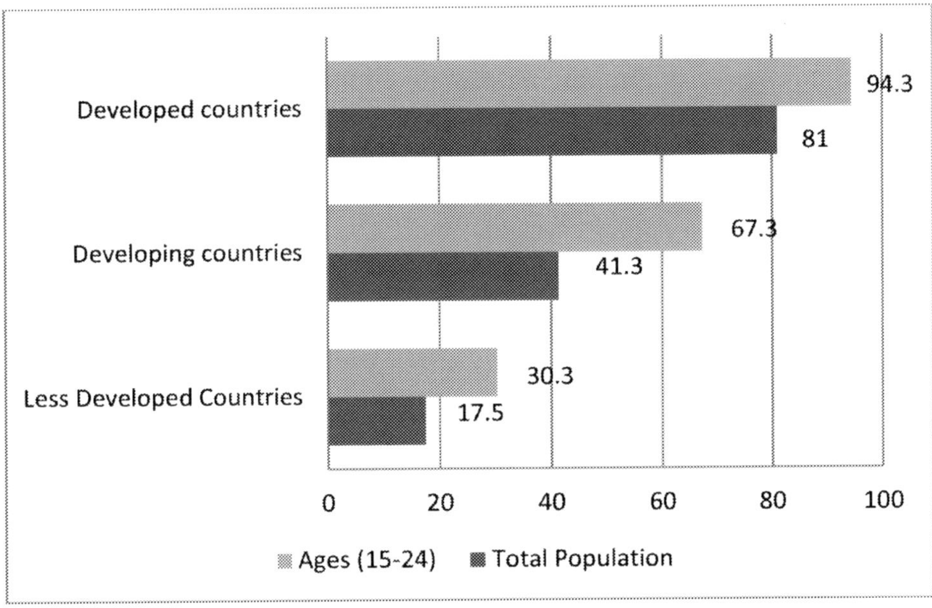

It is essential to understand importance of social media users age as specifically youth in this case is seen as the moving force for internationalization and globalization in the nearest future. In less than a single generation billions of people who had no access to the Internet were connected to global cyberspace. The majority of these new digital citizens are youth between 18-29. Already, two thirds of global Internet users are under the age of 35 and half are under the age of 25. Youth across the globe represent the largest demographic group online, and this is particularly true in Africa, the Middle East and Asia where they are connecting in record numbers. Virtually all of North America and Western Europe are already wired. The next wave of digital connectivity will occur in less developed and conflict-affected countries such as Bangladesh, Chad, the Democratic Republic of the Congo, Myanmar, and Somalia.

With respect to social media, there were 2.79 billion active users of social media in 2017. More than 75 percent of them were young people.

It is a generation that is as much online as they are offline. Globally, 92 percent of young people report going online at least once a day and 56 percent go online several times a day. Youth's connection to social media and online platforms is generating new communication channels and innovative paths for social interaction.

This young population represents tremendous potential to be used by businesses to go global, peace mediators for peace-building etc. Often, youth are considered as either passive and uninterested actors or as groups at high risk. However, youth are also an active asset to promote peace, development and security.

The UN promotes positions that youth is an essential and effective partners in promoting peace, sustainability, economic growth. That means engaging youth in a way that considers them as beneficiaries, partners and leaders in promoting peace and security. It also means providing them with access to spaces and channels to voice their opinions share their experiences and jointly plan for a better future.

In March 2018, the United Nations Department of Political Affairs (UNDPA), together with three Switzerland-based organizations – Swiss Peace, the Centre for Humanitarian Dialogue (HD) and Diplo Foundation – initiated the #Cyber Mediation Initiative.[4] The Initiative helps to better understand and leverage new technologies in global governance and collective security in the context of the Secretary-General's Strategy on New Technologies.

Moreover such Peace tech initiatives can be used by youth to enhance peace and security:[5]

1. **Data Collection, Processing and Analysis:** This category of Peace tech actors were some of the first to appear. It includes the collection of data to produce a series of online tools that support conflict early warning, promote greater transparency in decision-making and enhance confidence in important processes such as elections.
2. **Peace Gaming:** Another category of Peace tech initiatives involves peace gaming. These range from simple online games to more complex role playing games that model real world experiences.

3. **Digital Citizen Journalism:** Blogging, You Tubing and online journalism represent a growing genre of Peace tech. While there is significant diversity in this genre, some such as #18daysinegypt, represent a new way of understanding and portraying historical developments.
4. **Online Activism and Open Source Software:** Online petitions, e-surveys, open-source software and social forums represents another active category of Peace tech initiatives.
5. **Cyber Defence and E-Literacy:** This category of Peace tech refers to initiatives that emphasize skills training and enhancing digital literacy.
6. **Virtual Mapping:** This category of Peace tech leverages Geographic Information Systems (GIS) to combat violence and promote peace.

UN Security Council Resolution (2015) on Youth, Peace and Security stresses on the importance of youth involvement in peace initiatives: "Today's generation of youth is the largest the world has ever known, and...young people often form the majority of the population of countries affected by armed conflict...Youth should actively be engaged in shaping lasting peace and contributing to justice and reconciliation...A large youth population presents a unique demographic dividend that can contribute to lasting peace and economic prosperity if inclusive policies are in place".

Taking into account all of the above mentioned, it can be defined that social media play in conflict prevention and peace promotion the following roles:

1. Brings together different groups to discuss issues.
2. Helps improve governance.
3. Increases knowledge of complex issues.
4. Provides early warning.
5. Outlet to express emotions.
6. Motivator for peace.

As we can see the importance of online media has grown dramatically in recent years. The main advantages for users are that they are always available, they focus on being up to date and they provide information for free.

It is essential to understand the role social media has nowadays in different areas of people lives. Brief overview given in the paper stresses on the importance of using social media by youth in the areas of defence and security. Although, defence and security can be understood not only from peace-building perspective, but also as customers security when social media are used by businesses. A special attention here should be paid to young generation as those who promote internationalization.

Nowadays social media platforms allow companies to improve their international market presence and reach potential clients all over the world. As a result, more companies, both big and small, start to utilise them in their internationalisation strategy. Companies can perform various business functions through social media, including marketing, market research, and online retailing. The potential value of this trend for companies is huge.

The main benefits of social media strategies for internationalisation include the huge exposure that company can generate, the relatively low costs associated with it, the possibilities for customer segmentation and targeting it provides and the market insight that can be gained from analysing consumers' online behaviour and interacting with them through social networks.

In conclusion, we stress on the importance of social media use in terms of security in different areas of life. Moreover a key component here is analysis of social media users from the age perspective. It is needed to do so in order to use social media in the most efficient way having understood that youth is the generation, having huge impact on internationalization.

REFERENCES

1. Reporters without Borders, 2016. Facing reality after the Euromaidan, the situation of journalists and media in Ukraine, Accessed at https://rsf.org/sites/default/files/journalists_and_media_in_ukraine_-_rsf_2016.pdf on 7 January 2019.
2. Buffer Marketing Library. 21 Top social media Sites to Consider Your Brand. Accessed at https://buffer.com/library/social-media-sites on 19 February 2019.
3. World Telecommunication/ICT Indicators Database 2018 (22nd Edition/January

2019). Accessed at https://www.itu.int/en/ITU-D/Statistics/Pages/publications/wtid.aspx on 2 February 2019.

4. Centre for Humanitarian Dialogue, 2018, Launch of the Cybermediation Initiative – New Technologies for Political Mediation: Opportunities and Risks. Accessed at https://www.hdcentre.org/updates/launch-of-the-cybermediation-initiative-new-technologies-for-political-mediation-opportunities-and-risks/ on 10 February 2019.
5. Farrah, Raouf, Boer, de John and Muggah, Robert, 2017, Digitally-enabled Peace and Security: Reflections for the Youth, Peace and Security Agenda. Accessed at https://www.youth4peace.info/system/files/2018-04/2.%20TP_Social%20Media_SecDev.pdf on 22 February 2019.

5

Impact of Social Media on Economic Security and the Recruitment Process of the Labour Market

Bartlomiej Kozak

1. Introduction

Year by year the use of social media among the population is growing very fast. A few years ago, social media was mainly used as a platform for socializing, exchanging photos, interesting information, gossip, or making new friends which at the beginning were virtual and moved into the real world. Currently, we can observe a very strong change in this area. Social media contacts enter in our lives more deeply and make a real impact on our lives. Not only young people, but also the older generation has begun to use social media as a way to create their image, not only in the social space, but also on the professional front. Community portals are used more and more as a place not only to spend time together in the virtual world, but also to create business groups, or spaces to work together and create new ideas and solutions for the business tasks.[1]

Social media, year by year, is visible in the process of recruitment of new employees and searching for a job. The younger the target group from which employees are recruited, the more often recruiters use social media. According to a report by Lee Hecht Harrison DBM in Poland, in 2016, more than 96 per cent of recruiters, seeking employees, used an account on LinkedIn in the recruitment process, and Facebook was used by up to 40 per cent. Interestingly, we can observe that within one year, the number of recruiters who declare that they have completed the employment process via social media has increased from 10 per cent to 89 per cent. So what is the impact of social media on the economic security of young people entering the labour market? I will try to answer this question in my article.

2. Recruiters in Social Media

The labour market in Poland is becoming more and more "the employee's market" which means that more often it is easier for a qualified employee to find a good job, than for company to find a well-qualified worker. Companies are growing faster, need new employees, often highly qualified, who could be involved in the company's development. The "millennium" youths are accustomed to the continuous presence "online" and the use of social media as a natural medium for contact with peers, to make friends or function in society. The public institutions in Poland are adapting to this situation, introducing the possibility of electronic handling of most official matters, such as communication with the tax office, social security institution, municipal office, and also enabling electronic submission of an application to obtain a personal ID or establishing a company via the Internet. In face of this situation, companies as well as people directly recruiting new employees are more and more often transferring the process of recruitment to the Internet, and thus to social media. Some of the largest employers worldwide utilize social networking platforms more than traditional career portals to recruit employees.

The use of social media is illustrated in the figure that follows, which presents the number of users over the last years and the forecast for the coming years.[2]

The team of Labour Market Consultants Lee Hecht Harrison DBM in Poland, in order to better understand the operation of recruitment processes in companies, conducted a survey on 301 people who are

Figure 1: Social Media Users (in billions)

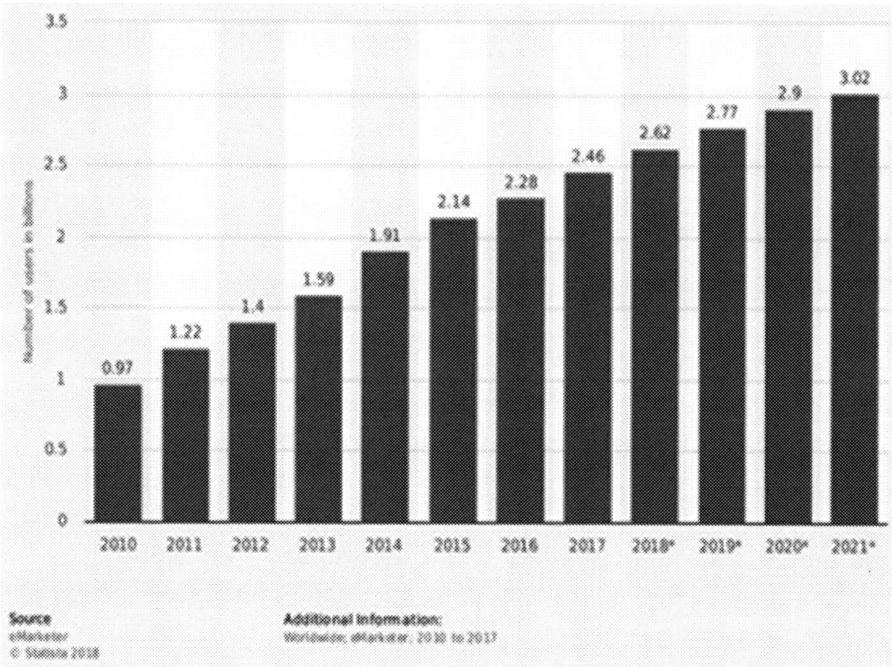

employees of personnel departments or companies specializing in recruitment processes. As part of the survey process, respondents were asked between 19 and 44 questions, which mainly focused on the workplace, the way of recruitment or the level of social media use in the recruitment process.

Sixty-two per cent of the surveyed people were employees of internal personnel departments in companies for which they recruit employees. Out of this group, as many as 79 per cent of people are employees of large companies that have over 250 people, 9 per cent are people from medium companies employing between 150 and 249 people, while 10 per cent of people work in companies employing between 25 and 149 people.

In this group, as many as 63 per cent of people were employees of foreign branches of corporations in Poland, while employees of Polish companies accounted for only 24 per cent of people and 13 per cent are people from Polish companies with foreign capital. Half of the respondents were employees of service companies, while the other half was almost equally divided among employees of production companies (26 per cent) and trade companies (24 per cent).

On the other hand, 38 per cent of respondents were people who work in recruitment companies, i.e. recruitment of employees for external entities. In this case, the picture is slightly different from the previous group. Fifty-two per cent of people are employees of companies dealing in professional services in the recruitment of employees who employ up to 25 people. Twenty-two per cent are people working in large head hunter corporations employing over 250 people. The remaining percentage were people employed in companies with between 25 and 149 employees (15 per cent) and people working in companies employing between 150 and 249 people (11 per cent). These companies most often seek specialists and temporary employees, and least frequently the management and specialists.

How are the recruiters presenting themselves on the web? According to research by Lee Hecht Harrison DBM, recruiters in Poland on an average hold 3.4 accounts in social networks. As many as 95 per cent of respondents have an account on LinkedIn and 96 per cent of account holders use this account in recruitment. The Polish equivalent of this business social networking portal, the Golden Line portal, there are 85 per cent accounts of which as much as 84 per cent use it in the recruitment process. It is a bit different in the case of Facebook, the account has 81 per cent of respondents, and only 40 per cent of recruiters use it for the recruitment process. The in-depth study shows that Facebook is seen largely as a portal to connect with friends and family through messages, posts and photos, which is why some recruiters avoid using the data collected there.

The use of social media by employees of HR departments is well illustrated in the chart that follows, where all social media platforms used by HR department employees were recorded.

Figure 2: The Use of Social Media by Employees of HR Departments in Recruitment

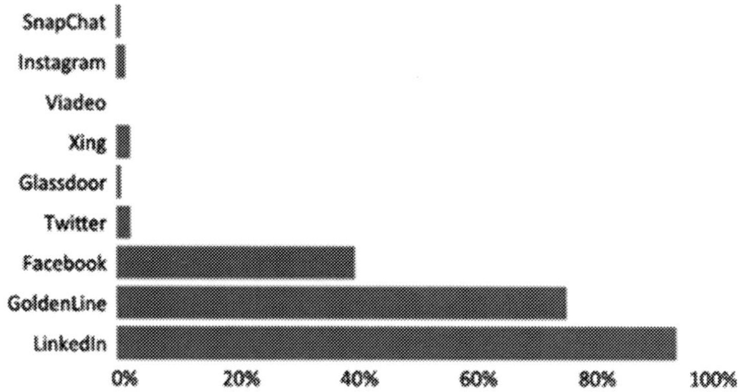

Source: Author's own compilation.

While employees of HR departments and employees of headhunters use LinkedIn to recruit employees, in the case of the Golden Line portal, employees of HH companies use it more and this percentage is above 80 per cent. Also, a slightly higher rate of use of Facebook for the recruitment process can be observed in HH employees. Details are presented in the graph that follows.

Figure 3: The Use of Social Media by Employees of Head Hunters in Recruitment

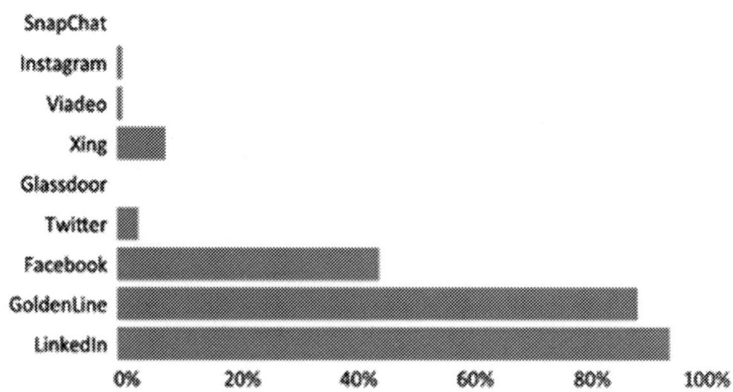

Source: Author's own compilation.

2.1. How often do recruiters use social media?

We could answer this question briefly: very often. Recruiters use social media quite a lot, and one could even say that it is an everyday tool for them. It is well illustrated in the figure that follows:

Figure 4: Recruiters Activity in Social Media

Source: Author's own compilation.

Thus, we see that as many as 95 per cent of all recruiters actively use social media in their daily work. And among headhunters' employees, this percentage is even higher and amounts to as much as 98 per cent.

It is also worth asking whether, in addition to social media activity, they use these media to conduct recruitment processes and have they been able to finalize the recruitment process using social media? This has been presented in the figure that follows:

Figure 5: Finalizing the Recruitment Process in Social Media by the Recruiter

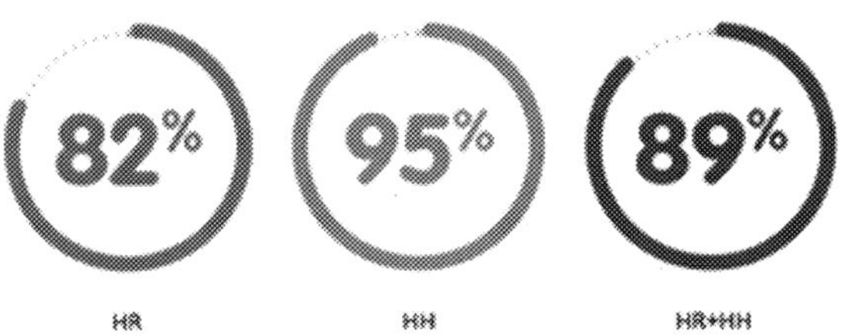

Source: Author's own compilation.

It turns out that up to 89 per cent of all recruiters surveyed in the previous year finalized the recruitment process with the use of social media. And among the employees of companies dealing exclusively with recruitment processes, this percentage is even higher and amounts to as much as 95 per cent. The new generation is constantly connected through social networks. Companies realise that the potential candidate pool is vast and growing daily online. Forward-thinking companies are investing in recruiting this new generation of workers. Younger generation will also prefer to seek employment through their natural environment, which means through social media that is an integral part of their lives.

3. Personal Image on the Web vs. Job Search

As the proverb says: "Fine feathers make fine birds", translating directly word by word form Polish language "how they see you, that they describe you". This maxim also works very well today in relation to our image on the web. What you post online can have a significant influence on your career. Young people often share photos or videos from their everyday lives, often posting materials that they would not necessarily share with their employers. Often the recruiters emphasize during trainings that the first action to be taken when preparing to look for a job is to review profiles in the social media in terms of the materials published there. The best justification for undertaking this action is the results of the survey, which shows that as many as 50 per cent of recruiters, verify candidates for work based on their private profiles in social media. This percentage is greater for employees of HR departments in the companies and is 52 per cent.

Figure 6: Verification of Candidates Based on Information from Private Profiles in Social Media

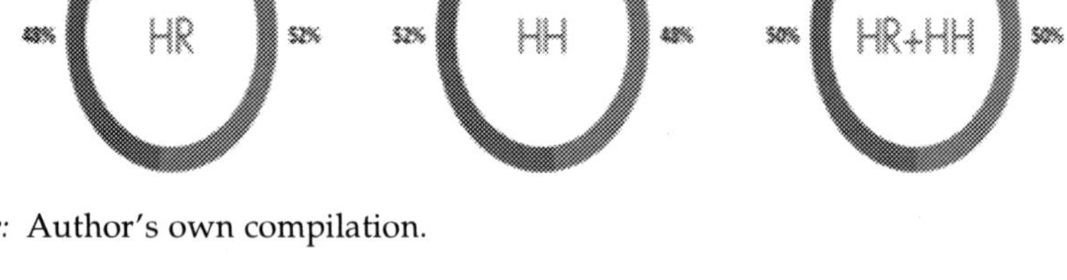

Source: Author's own compilation.

As can be seen in the above charts, half of the recruiters verify private profiles in social media. However, do they make a decision based on the information obtained in this way? You might be surprised but more often the information available about people in the network determines their employment. In 2015, the percentage of recruiters who based their recruitment on information from social media and considered whether it is worth employing a candidate was up to 50 per cent, and a year later, this percentage increased to 62 per cent.

Figure 7: Undertaking the Employment of People after Verification of their Social Profile

Source: Author's own compilation.

This indicator, as you can see, is higher every year. This can be a warning signal for all those who have a very loose approach to posting information about their private life in social media. Bearing in mind that some recruiters do not want to admit that they are verifying private profiles of candidates as part of the recruitment process, the impact of how we create our image on the web can play an important role in our professional lives. We can even observe that this percentage is higher, and amounts to 66 per cent, in the case of recruiters from headhunters' companies.

Figure 8: Undertaking the Employment of People after Verification of their Social Profile

Source: Author's own compilation.

We know how numerous a groups of recruiters who doubt candidates assessed in the recruitment process, based on materials on their profiles. However, did they reject the candidates on the basis of the information they were acquainted with? It turns out that this percentage, fortunately, is not that big, but it is still big. On average, as many as 27 per cent of recruiters rejected the candidate's application based on information that could be found about him/her on the web. Among the employees of recruitment companies, this percentage was even higher and amounted to 29 per cent. The details of the test are presented in the figure that follows.

Figure 9: Recruiters Who Rejected the Candidacy-based on Data from Social Media

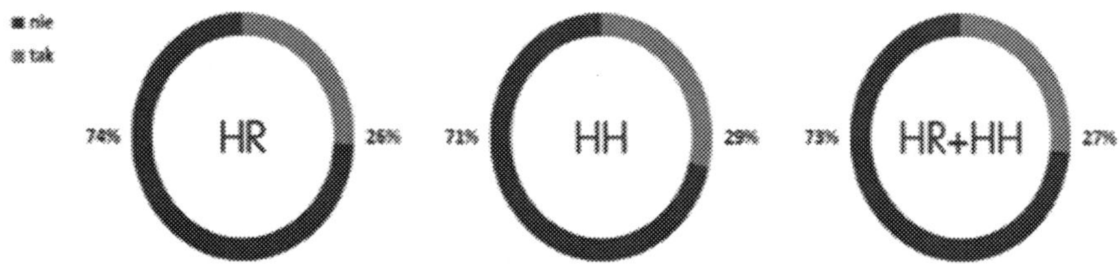

Source: Author's own compilation.

So this trend will continue and the recruiters will pay more attention to your online presence. Yes!

Figure 10: The Willingness of Recruiters to Encourage the Use of Social Media at Work

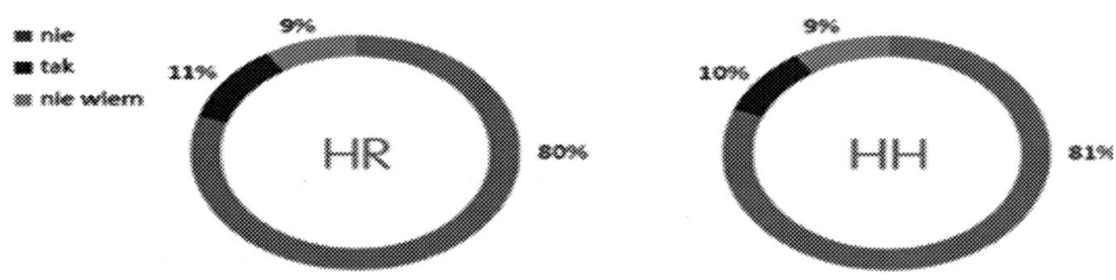

Source: Author's own compilation.

4. Social Media as an Image Building Tool

Nowadays, companies are increasingly aware of the need to not only skillfully choose methods that enable them to verify prospective candidates, but have alsostarted to create a positive image of themselves on the web. Only 1 per cent of respondents declared that their company does not use any form of image promotion on the Internet. Over 81 per cent of the respondents declared that their company has a website with a separate career page, while 12 per cent have a website without it. In the case of employees of internal HR departments, this total value amounted to as much as 97 per cent (94 per cent webpage with career page and 3 per cent webpage without a career tab). In addition, as many as 44 per cent of respondents confirmed that their company has a mobile version of the website.

Companies, in their efforts to gain popularity and trust among future employees, also build their image in social media. Over 60 per cent of companies have at least one profile on a social media platform. Most often it is LinkedIn—used by 69 per cent of people, the next portal is Facebook, where 65 per cent of entities have their accounts. On the third place is the Golden Line portal, where every second company has its profile. The fourth position is also worth highlighting, the profile on the website pracuj.pl (translate to work.pl), which is the most popular portal that brings together job offers mainly from the Polish market, which has as many as 42 per cent of companies.

Being aware that the company's presence in the network cannot only rely on the establishment of a profile on social media, as many as 90 per cent of companies decided to hire an employee who helps them build an image on the web. Most often these people are those in the department dealing with communication, marketing and PR (65 per cent) as part of the company's organizational chart, while they are less often employees of the human resources department (17 per cent).[3]

4.1. Leading Industries are Moving Towards Mobility

When analysing the "We Are Social Singapore"[4] report in 2014, the number of queries for search engines from mobile devices exceeded the number of inquiries from desktop devices. In Poland, this indicator was reached in 2016, when the number of searches from mobile devices amounted to 51 per cent of all queries. By analogy, this trend has also moved to the level associated with the search for a new job. At the same time, when in Poland searches from mobile devices exceeded searches from desktop devices, according to the Jobvite report, almost 20 per cent of Americans were looking for a new job through Facebook.[5] That is why companies in Poland have started emphasising on development of their brand on the Internet. As mentioned in the previous paragraph, 44 per cent of companies had a mobile version of their website at the end of 2016, and another 42 per cent implemented such a solution in 2017.[6]

Based on the study by Lee Hecht Harrison DBM in Poland,[7] the 5 most-represented industries in the study were analyzed. These were Finance, IT/R&D, FMCG, Pharmacy and Retail. It was analyzed whether companies from these particular industries have been using social media in the recruitment process. The results of these tests are presented in the figure that follows.

Figure 11: The Use, Ever, of Social Media in the Recruitment of Employees in Particular Industries

Source: Author's own compilation.

As we can see in the above figure, all surveyed companies in 'IT and R&D' and the financial industry declare that they have been using social media in the recruitment process. At a slightly lower level, 88-89 per cent, the use of online communication channels is declared by representatives of the FMCG industry, related to the sale or trading in fast-moving goods intended for sale in supermarkets.

It is also worth noting that all companies in the industry referred to as 'sales' declare that they at least once hired an employee through social media. In the second place there are companies from the IT/R&D industry, where the index is 93 per cent. Details are presented in Figure 12.

They were also asked how they use social media to carry out recruitment processes. As many as 84 per cent of respondents used this

Figure12: Employment, an Employee through Social Media at least once

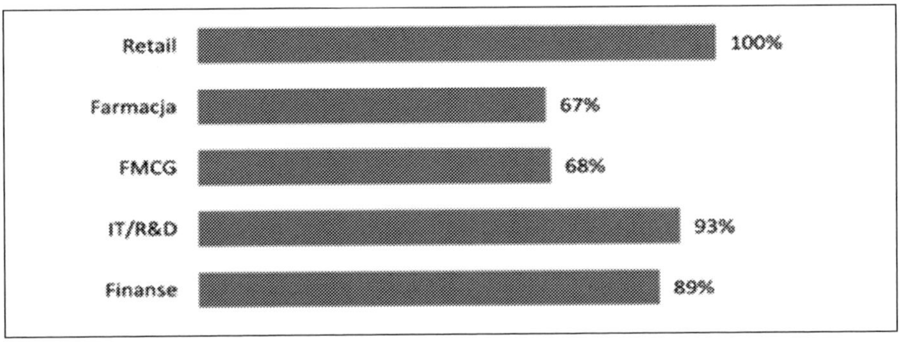

Source: Author's own compilation.As we can see on the above charts, companies from all analyzed industries very actively used social media during the recruitment process of new employees.

channel to contact candidates—in this group, 100 per cent of the company from the retail sector admitted that they used social media as a way of communication in the recruitment process. Other industries in this area declared contact with the candidates at the following level: Pharmaceutical 67 per cent, financial 86 per cent, FMCG 73 per cent, IT / R & D 79 per cent. Another, equally high indicator has reached indications regarding the use of social media in recruitment of employees by 'direct search' method, which means: direct recruitment of employees with high qualification in the labour market, who do not seek employment themselves. In this case, the rate was 81 per cent, and divided into particular industries: Pharmaceutical 78 per cent, Financial 82 per cent, FMCG 77 per cent, IT/R&D 86 per cent, Retail 75 per cent.

On the third place, with the result of 65 per cent, there was a declaration of companies using social media for the publication of paid job offers, and divided into particular industries: Pharmaceutical 78 per cent, Financial 64 per cent, FMCG 73 per cent, IT/R&D 43 per cent, Retail 50 per cent.

It is also worth analysing the usage of social media by particular industries. It is valuable information for both: companies that by entering given market want to be visible online through social media platforms, and also it is valuable information for people who will know where to find the best industry information for them, when they are looking for job offers in a given profession. In the survey, LinkedIn gained the most interest, 95 per cent, Golden Line 81 per cent and Facebook 77 per cent. These indications are presented in Figure 13.

Figure 13: The Use of Social Media by Companies from Specific Industries

	LinkedIn	GoldenLine	Facebook	Twitter	Glassdoor	Xing	Viadeo	Instagram	SnapChat	Inne
Farmaceutyczna / Medyczna	100%	62%	62%	15%	8%	15%	0%	31%	0%	0%
Finansowa	89%	84%	76%	11%	3%	5%	0%	24%	11%	3%
FMCG	90%	77%	77%	16%	3%	0%	0%	26%	16%	3%
IT / RD	100%	89%	78%	22%	6%	6%	0%	33%	6%	0%
Retail	92%	77%	85%	15%	0%	0%	0%	23%	15%	0%
Średnio	95%	81%	77%	16%	4%	5%	1%	23%	10%	2%

It is worth mentioning that all companies from the pharmaceutical industry and IT / R & D are using LinkedIn. Whereas the Golden Line portal is the most popular among institutions from the IT / R & D sector (89 per cent) and financial (84 per cent). Interestingly, the Facebook portal is the most popular in the industry related to the sale, the so-called Retail (85 per cent). In addition to the top social networking portals, Instagram is also worth paying attention to, which is used by almost every fourth company (23 per cent).

4.2. Social Media in the Manufacturing, Commercial and Service Industries

The use of social media in the service or commercial industry is becoming more and more popular every year, and the use of this communication channel is treated more and more as a natural way of contacting with customers. How is the use of these media in the production industry presented in this context? Analyzing data from the Lee Hecht Harrison DBM report in Poland, we can see that the use of social media for business purposes, is declared by 86 per cent of companies. Most companies using the latest communication channels operate in the service industry - 89 per cent, followed by the trade sector (85 per cent) and then the manufacturing industry at 83 per cent.

Figure 14: The Use of Social Media for Business Purposes in Specific Industries

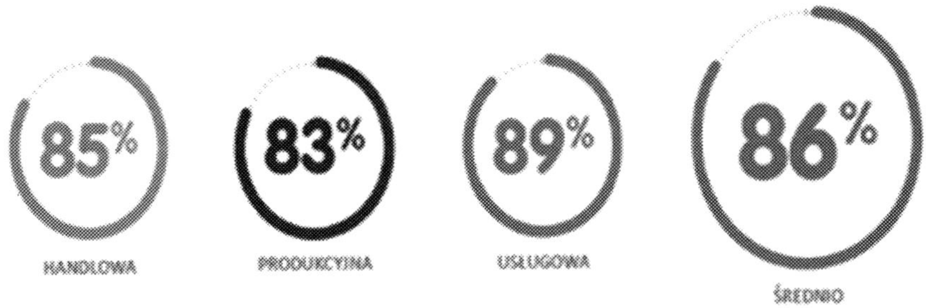

We can therefore observe that the use of social media in particular industries is at a similar level, and also in the case of the manufacturing industry it is significant. It is worth comparing this with data on the use of social media in the recruitment process. This data is shown in the figure that follows.

Figure 15: The Use of Social Media in Recruitment of Employees in Particular Industries

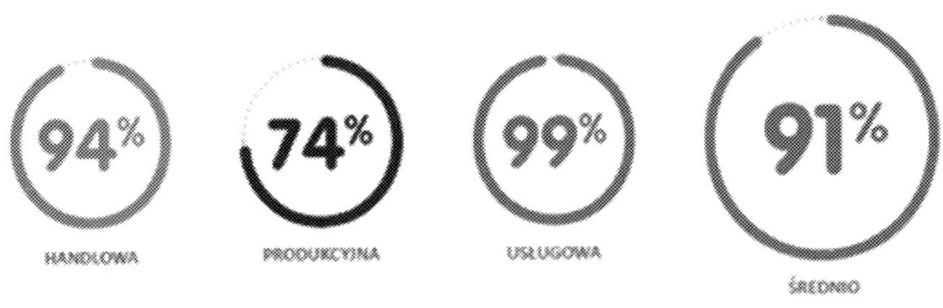

When comparing data on the use of social media in the recruitment process, we get information that on an average up to 91 per cent of institutions have used this way to recruit employees. Most often, this communication channel was used by service companies, where only 1 per cent of respondents in this area did not use this form of contact. In the trade sector, this indicator was slightly lower and amounted to 94 per cent. However, in the case of the industry sector, the use of social media for the recruitment process was declared by 74 per cent of companies. Being aware of the fact that while service and commercial companies are increasingly using social media to promote their products, it is natural to use these media to attract new employees. In the case of the production industry, these companies often deal with the production of products that do not go directly to the end customer, and are only a component of more complex elements, e.g. cars, computers, etc. Therefore, looking from the point that 74 per cent of companies have been using social media to recruit employees, we can say that this percentage is at a very high level, and the company's awareness of the modern way of communication is very high.

A very good test of the information presented above and putting it into real activities of companies is to compare them with data on real employment in companies, thanks to the use of social media. The respondents were asked if they were hiring through social networks. The results of this study are presented in the figure below.

Figure 16: Real Employee Employment Thanks to Social Media

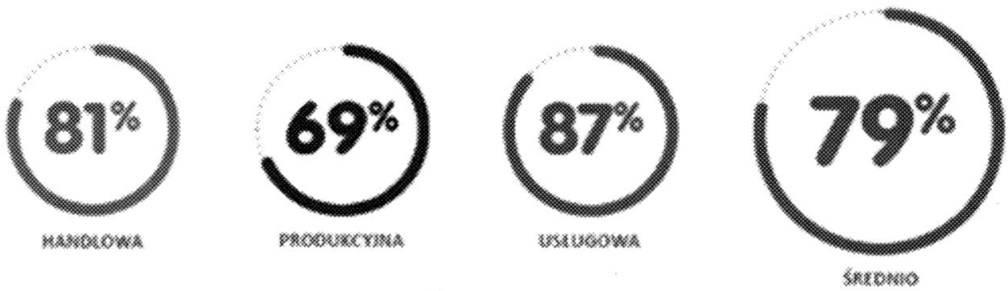

As we can see in the above Figure that on an average 79 per cent of companies from the analyzed industries confirmed that they were able to employ an employee through the use of social media. The highest rate in this aspect was achieved by service companies, in which this level amounted to as much as 87 per cent, however, the production companies also obtained a very optimistic result of 69 per cent in this matter. We can observe a very interesting relationship here, that only 5 per cent of manufacturing companies that used social media in the recruitment process did not employ an employee based on such activities. Therefore, it can be stated that the presence of companies in social media translates well into the acquisition of employees by this way.

Social Media as a Recruitment Tool

The use of social media in the recruitment process is increasingly perceived positively by recruiters. Recruiters also begin to appreciate the advantages noted from their point of view, such as the increase in the number of candidates applying for a given position, which was indicated by 63 per cent of employees in HR departments in HR companies and as much as 79 per cent of employees seeking professional employees (HH). Another benefit noted by recruiters is the shortening of the recruitment time, which is noticed by 48 per cent of HR employees and 68 per cent of HH employees. Social media and their way of functioning make searching for new employees more effective, but also cheaper—what was emphasized by 52 per cent of HR recruiters and 60 per cent of HH recruiters.

However, these factors are not indicated as the greatest benefits from the use of social media in the recruitment and search for new employees. It turns out that the biggest advantage, according to both employees from HR departments (81 per cent) and HH (79 per cent), is the opportunity to reach passive candidates. These people seemingly do not look for work and do not browse portals with job offers. However, if they encounter an interesting job offer on social media or contact a person who, based on information obtained from their social profile, will offer them a job they are ready to take up the challenge and are consider changing their job. This situation has been used effectively recently in Poland by the company 'pracuj.pl', which is the largest portal presenting job offers. The company runs a large-scale promotional campaign on social media, which in a slightly exaggerated way presents the faults of the superiors in the company, suggesting to the disgusted employees "check if you are not looking for" (new job).

Through presence on social media, companies improve their image among future employees and people who could be interested in the jobs offered by the company in the future. This is not a disinterested activity because, as the recruiters note (46 per cent HR and 21 per cent HH), thanks to the presence in the network, the company's image is improved among both: social media and general. This also translates into the quality of candidates applying to given companies, as indicated by 35 per cent of recruiters from HR departments and 36 per cent of recruiters from headhunters.

A summary of all the above information is presented in Table 1.

Table 1: Various Aspects of Social Media as a Recruitment Tool

Feature	*Recruiters from HR departments (%)*	*Recruiters from HH companies (%)*
Increase in the number of candidates	63	79
Shortening the recruitment time	48	68
Saving costs	52	60
Reaching passive candidates	81	79
Improving the quality of candidates	35	36
The increase of employee recommendation	16	19
Improving the company's image	46	21
Other	2	2
I do not see any	1	1

4.4. An Ideal Profile—Information that the Recruiters Pay Attention to

Despite how much you can talk about the 'employee but not the employer market', it is still and probably always will remain that for the best job offer candidates will always have to work hard to get them. Therefore, it is important that the information contained in the online portfolio is valuable and able to attract the attention of the recruiter.

Practice, practice and once again practice. This is how you could summarize information about what is the most important feature for employers. As many as 80 per cent of recruiters from HR departments and from HH companies point out that the most important feature of the candidate is their professional experience. It is therefore important to start gaining valuable professional experience as soon as possible, as it will be the key to success at a later time. It is also worth noting that the professional experience presented in our profile should be continuous (does not have gaps) and consistent with the information contained in the CV sent to the employer.

The second very important feature emphasized by recruiters is knowledge of foreign languages. This skill is valued by 3 out of 4 headhunters and every second recruiter from the HR department. What the companies, both small and large, emphasize is that knowledge of foreign languages is crucial for them, because it requires a long period of time to acquire such skills, and almost all other skills required for a given job position the company is able to teach in a short period of time.

Another important and the most desirable feature for a candidate are skills that match those that are crucial for a given job position. An added value is the confirmation of our skills in the form of "reference" given on the professional profile, which our workers and supervisors give us. Such information is positively perceived by 44 per cent of recruiters.[8]

5. Summary

It would be possible to make many comparisons showing the features most wanted by the recruiters and to conduct many discourses on the advantages and disadvantages of being online. The truth, however, is that social media has become part of our everyday lives. They are a way to communicate with our friends and allow us to maintain relationships both private and professional. Their conscious use will contribute to increasing the level of economic security and the ability to find a place in the labour market. Virtually every action in the network creates our image. It is, therefore, worthwhile to deliberately decide what image we create and what our plan for professional development looks like, which we will gradually implement.

The data presented above can clearly demonstrate that social media has become a part of our lives. As with our life outside the network, our actions and decisions affect our professional development, opportunities to gain attractive employment and provide ourselves with economic security, similarly it happens in case of our life in the virtual world, which in the non-virtual and real way contribute to shape our everyday life.

REFERENCES

1. Rekrutacja w mediach spo³ecznoœciowych (socialrecruiting) Joanna Palonka, Teresa Porêbska-Mi¹c
2. Jak media spo³ecznoœciowe zmieni³y rynek pracy (How Social media havechangedlabour market), Andrzej Zieliñski, http://www.tajemnicekariery.pl/media-spolecznosciowe-a-rynek-pracy/
3. Profesjonalne i eksperckie media spo³ecznoœciowe a rynek pracy,(Professional and expertSocial media and the labor market) Izabela Maria Stefaniak, 2016

4. http://www.slideshare.net/wearesocialsg/digital-in-2016/329
5. http://www.jobvite.com/wp-content/uploads/2016/03/Jobvite_Jobseeker_Nation_2016.
6. GoldenLine, 2017, *Co czeka bran¿ê HR w 2017 roku?(What awaits the HR industry in 2017?)*
7. Lee Hecht Harrison DBM w Polsce, Raport media spo³ecznoœciowe w rekrutacji, 2017 (Lee Hecht Harrison DBM in Poland, Social media report in recruitment, 2017).
8. Czy wykorzystanie mediów spo³ecznoœciowych w HR zmienia siê tak szybko jak rynek pracy?(Does the use of Social media in HR change as quickly as the labour market?) Magdalena Tyburcy, 2017, www.dbm.pl

6

Rise of Social Media and Its Impact on Peace and Security

Dr. Pradeep Kumar and Daria Szczepańska

Introduction

Thanks to this ease of access, we can know about major events as they unfold, even before the mainstream media has a chance to report on it. Such a quick spread of information can be beneficial in, fe: alerting others, taking necessary precautions, or awareness in general. It is very important to consider the nature of social networking and how it has taken a foothold in today's society; it has become quite popular to access knowledge via social media. Worry of having profiles on those platforms is how people can "dox" others—share private information (home address, phone numbers, email, places of employment, etc) as a means of either intimidation or simply ruining the lives of other people. Doxxing has been used mainly by fringe political groups from the left and right, but also for non-political means. Regardless of its intent, this had major repercussions on security and peace. The worst uses of social media, however, have been those utilised by terrorist organisations, such as the Islamic State of Iraq and Syria (ISIS). By using accounts on various platforms, these terror organisations recruited more people for their cause, despite major measures by the companies to crack down on such groups. Not everything about social media is bad news, however. There have been countless reports of how awareness of important issues has spread with the use of social media. Examples could be the Black Lives Matter movement, which highlighted disproportionate police brutality among the African-American community in the United States. The use of hashtags to popularise trends has alerted others to the issues that are ongoing in modern society. Events that are organised on Facebook have had large numbers of people showing up to protest what they perceived as injustices happening; these protests in turn pushed politicians to make serious legislative changes to ensure peace and stability. The main goal of this paper is to give examples of how the rise of social media has impacted peace and security, both on a local and international level. Discussed will both be the positive and adverse effects of how social media has left its print in how prosperity can either be promoted or undermined.

The Different Social Media Platforms and how they Influenced Society

Before we discuss, how social media affects societal well-being, it is worth to get the reader to know what social media platforms are the ones that leave behind most imprint on this topic. There are many companies that allow Internet users to sign up and create their accounts, and each service has a different functionality. Because of that, the precise effect each platform has is also worth diving into. Below are some of the biggest social media providers, their background (date of foundation, functionality) and how it generally influenced world events, for better or for worse.

Facebook: Undoubtedly the most popular and widespread social media platform, Facebook has over 2,5 billion active users, a very large chunk of the population is connected to this platform, Facebook was founded by Mark Zuckerberg in February 2004. A social networking site, where users create and customise their profiles, share content and connect with other users, it has overtaken the previous networking giant MySpace in 2008 and has grown into one of the biggest companies in the world. In addition to people creating their own personal profiles, users can create pages dedicated to anything from musicians to political groups, the latter of which will be discussed in detail later on. Verified users (those who are actually owned by the people/group they claim to be) have millions of followers, and they too can share content and communicate with their users. Also, Facebook has the Messenger application, in which Facebook (FB for short) members can send instant messages to others. Although taking pride in supporting the easy flow of information between its users, FB has been under criticism for years, sometime sin highly publicised events. One of the most repeated criticisms is the fact that FB does not offer complete privacy online; resulting in personal data being available to supranational entities and surveillance programs, such as Cambridge Analytica and PRISM. The most severe criticism Facebook has gained, however, was for its inability to effectively monitor content that is published. Many instances of hate speech, racism, promotion of radical groups, live streaming violent acts and, most importantly, fake news, have been left unchecked, which culminated in Mark Zuckerberg being heard during a US Congressional trial. In turn, this has caused Facebook to implement a stricter policy regarding content sharing. On the other hand, due to instant messaging and the ability to create and organise events on FB, people have been able to come in groups to protest injustices and to promote nonviolent means for political problems. A prime example of that would be the Parkland High School shooting, the aftermath of which was a giant protest against gun violence and push for restrictive measures for gun control. The protest originated on Facebook and obtained worldwide coverage.

Twitter: Created as a microblogging platform in 2006, Twitter currently has 320 million active users. It operates on the basis of "tweets" - short, public messages to other users, with a limited count of 280 characters per tweet. Tweets are ranked in visibility due to the popularity of a trending hashtag (#), trends are dependent on the amounts of tweets posted with the hashtag over a period of time. Twitter has been a major player in affecting world events through tweets. By organising protests, sometimes referred to as "Twitter Revolutions", it has led to major happenings, such as the 2013 Turkish protests, 2011 Egyptian revolution, for example. Often used as a means of spreading awareness of a situation, Twitter has been treated as an alternative news source and is used by major world figures, such as Donald Trump and Pope Francis, to communicate with followers, giving updates on current events. As with Facebook, however, Twitter comes with a downside. Titled "Twitter mobs", groups of people have been harassing their opponents through the use of Twitter by tweeting to others, inciting them to be "cancelled", or taken down and doxxed. Utilised by political groups from the left and right, this has sparked a considerable worry about the privacy of users and the inability of Twitter's moderators on taking down harmful material. Material that may include also fake news, which could be spread very quickly, or even propaganda of terrorist organisations. ISIS has had many accounts that enticed others to join their ranks. Swift measures to undermine such promotion of hatred, violence and misinformation, were imposed, such as blocking certain hashtags from being tweeted or with tweets being deleted that contain the harmful hashtag. Despite its ability to quickly inform and mobilise users to protest and engage in civil disobedience, many governments weren't too fond of it: Twitter is banned in countries like China, North Korea, Iran, with blocks to access happening in Egypt, Turkey, Venezuela, among other places. It is safe to say that countries who wish to have authoritarian control of their citizens are not too fond of Twitter.

YouTube: Since its inception in 2005, YouTube has become the largest video sharing network in the world, with millions of videos uploaded daily for over 1,3 billion users. The premise behind YouTube is to share either user-made content or the one that already existed. This allows users to spread their knowledge and messages to a very wide audience. but not only that. YouTube has become a source of alternative news media, with some "amateur" channels surpassing mainstream media channels in terms of viewership and subscriptions. While YouTube has a policy that deletes videos of pornographic, brutal, and racist content, there are many channels that promote hatred of people from different beliefs; one infamous case that caused worldwide rage and protests was the 2012 short film *Innocence of Muslims,* which caused protests that resulted in deaths. Videos that promote conspiracy theories and fake news, have, like the previous platforms described here, caused division and furthered the spread of misinformation. Additionally, YouTube was utilised as a platform to upload extremist group's propaganda, but due to working with law enforcement, those responsible were quickly caught. Being an alternative source of news doesn't have to be a bad thing, however, and having so many viewers can be a plus. Ordinary citizens can easily show the world at large that their governments are being oppressive, and this could result in international debates, as it has happened. The ability to spread a message of peace via video is a powerful tool, as we will discuss later on.

Instagram: The last major social media platform to be discussed in this segment will be Instagram, the largest photo and video sharing networking site, having nearly 27 million active users. Also utilising hashtags to have a wider reach on its servers, Instagram users can use the platform either for private users or for public means, often for social awareness. Imagery is extremely strong and now many activists are using Instagram as a messaging tool to distribute their message far and large, encouraging many to get active. It also offers prominent people direct access to their supporters to offer undiluted messages. One example would be the #postboxselfie hashtag in Australia, where users posted photos with the hashtag during the nationwide referendum for marriage equality. Also, #blacklivesmatter was used by celebrities to spread awareness of the issue. Sadly, Instagram is also host to many users who post hateful content. Both the far left and far right band together to dox people they do not disagree with and post images that distort the truth in their favour. Oftentimes, such accounts go unnoticed until they are reported, allowing them to stay on the internet for longer periods of time. The above examples given are just a few of many, but these are the primary examples with the widest audiences. Since there are many views of the world as there are people, it is worth focusing on those who have had a more positive influence by using social media.

Social Media as a Means to Influence Peace and Security

Oftentimes the mainstream media and academia point towards everything wrong with social media: from its mental effects on the youth to how it can lead to violence. This is not without reason, and there is a need to tackle the disruptive elements which could target vulnerable people to create havoc in the peaceful co-existence of mankind. 1Such forms of networking have major societal, economic and political ramifications. In addition to providing alternate ways to access news, knowledge and entertainment, social networking platforms provide those means to spread a certain message and to push for change. In 2010-2011, one major event was dubbed as the first "social media revolution".

The Arab Spring: Beginning in Tunisia, the Arab Spring was a wave of demonstrations, protest and revolutions that swept the Arab world between 2010 and 2012. Caused by many factors, including opposition to authoritarianism, a demand for democracy, secularism and equal rights, it affected all countries in North Africa and in the Middle East to one extent or another. The protests had many forms, from civil disobedience to violent riots. Unfortunately, in three cases, the Arab Spring resulted in three civil wars: the Libyan Civil War, the Iraqi insurgency and the Syrian Civil War, all are ongoing as of 2020. In few instances, the governments collapsed and were replaced with new ones, and some states saw no changes within them. While the outcome of the Arab Spring cannot be strictly defined as either positive or negative, it is without a doubt that social media played a role in how these events unfolded. The scale of how large was the contribution of social media in these demonstrations is still a matter of debate. Nevertheless, the world witnessed for the first time how social media https://www.socialbakers.com/blog/social-media-platforms-during-coronavirus 1 can be "weaponized" to fight for justice; the media focused heavily on young protesters mobilising in the streets in political opposition, smartphones in hand. 2Online networks were critical for the coordination of a core group of activists, especially in Egypt. In the demonstrations, civil society leaders in Arab countries stressed the position of "the Internet, cell phones and social networking." In addition, the Arab nations have used new media to practice freedom of speech and as a platform for public participation. Online networking and electronic messaging have played a significant role in transforming abstract concepts into collective practice. Mohamed Bouazizi's photos-the street vendor whose self-immolation ignited the protests—spread rapidly online via family and friends networks. Once the governments began cracking down on protesters, videos and images showing the brutality of law enforcement dealing with the demonstrations spread like wildfire and quickly gained the attention of international media outlets, and then to governmental and non-governmental organisations globally. The methods of organising the civil riots were through the use of Twitter and Facebook for the most part. By organising events on Facebook, large amounts of people knew when to show up, what was the goal of the protest, and the number of attendees. Through Twitter, people knew immediately about what was the newest bit of information and the newest organised protests. Videos shared on YouTube were watched by millions around the globe and re-shared by global news networks, further spreading awareness. For better or for worse, the Arab Spring bolstered social media as a tool to organise and spread information about the societies people live in. While it could be disputed that the Arab Spring has done more harm than good, it was the first time when networking sites were utilised to show the world that not everything is as mainstream media portrays reality to be.

Gismondi (2014) notes that a study in Washington found that social media helped to shape and lead the debate with regard to the politics of the Arab Spring, and that young and educated people tended to lead this discourse, with women also being highly involved with social media participation—which is worth mentioning, knowing that women have limited rights in Arab nations. It appears, however, that claiming that social networking sparked the uprisings may be a misunderstanding, because the demonstrations continued in Egypt. Social networking, though, is simply a method for the quick and effective distribution of information—in almost the same manner as leaflets and published manifestos have been https://www.journalism.org/2012/11/28/role-social-media-arab-uprisings/ 2 used for ages.

Corona Virus Outbreak 2020

This is an ongoing topic as of writing this essay, as such; the complete assessment cannot be made. What conclusions can be drawn as of now are the ones that stem through the use of social media as the pandemic continues to spread. The COVID-19 pandemic, which originated in China, has now spread to all parts of the globe, currently causing one of the biggest disruptions of all aspects of global life. From everyday routines to governmental procedures, the coronavirus pandemic has affected much of the globe's population, even if the people themselves did not get sick. Such an upheaval to every part of the world's functions has, of course, had an impact on how social media has picked up on it, and how it was used to inform others of the threat to their security. Despite such a broad spectrum of obligation and overwhelming control over the dissemination of content, several outlets are trying to do what they can to provide aid, including pledging to fund humanitarian operations, taking action to halt the spread of fake news, and giving guidance to businesses. Various social media platforms took it upon 3 themselves to raise awareness of the coronavirus, but also to warn against misinformation that has spread throughout social media, like any other major world event. Facebook might get a bad reputation for doing little in the past to prevent the spread of fake news, but Mark Zuckerberg, the CEO, informed that FB is monitoring the content published by its users, with the help of their regional offices. Fact checks are implemented and users are warned if a bit of information is fake news. Along with the review of information, Facebook also promotes content from credible sources, such as news networks and academic research centres. These steps are important to follow, as users turn to social media for news first and foremost. Apart from strictly Internet actions, Facebook has donated over 700,000 face masks and pledged to donate $145 million dollars for healthcare providers and small-scale business owners. Other examples of how social media platforms are helping out to make people aware of the necessary precautions are many. For example, Instagram promotes self-isolation with hashtags (such as "#stayathome") and stickers for photos; celebrities and other influencers were quick to grasp on this and as such, Instagram's algorithms help to promote content that https://www.socialbakers.com/blog/social-media-platforms-during-coronavirus 3 highlights the importance of staying at home and being cautious during the pandemic. The messaging platform WhatsApp has launched an information hub for COVID-19, helping users be up to date with the newest information regarding the coronavirus. On top of that, WhatsApp has a chatbot which answers concerns from users and also acts as a deterrent to the spread of misinformation. As a last example, Messenger has connected itself to public organisations, where in turn they can directly communicate to people, sending news updates and warnings, should the need arise.

Black Lives Matter

A movement that originated in the United States, Black Lives Matter came about in 2013, after the acquittal of George Zimmerman, who shot and killed Trayvon Martin, an Afro-American youth. After two more instances of white police officers being cleared of charges after fatal shootings of two other Afro-American teenagers, the movement emerged as a coalition of various minority groups in the USA to highlight the injustices they face on an everyday basis. Founded by community organisers Alicia Garza and Opal Tometi, Black Lives Matter spread on social media with the hashtag containing the organisation's name. Many media figures, from sport stars, celebrities and liberal politicians used the hashtag to further extend the reach of the message. In fact, former US president Barack Obama made an indirect mention of the BLM movement, saying "Trayvon Martin could have been my son. Another way of saying that is Trayvon Martin could have been me 35 years ago". Such was the impact of BLM, which it extended beyond US borders, having several chapters in other countries. Due to social media use to communicate the issue of police brutality and unequal treatment of minorities in the United States, it started a nationwide debate on how police officers should conduct when apprehending potential criminals. Videos online that showed law enforcement treating people's colour in a discriminatory way were recorded by bystanders; this prompted the police to equip its personnel with body cameras so no abuse of power goes unpunished. Events to organise communities into protests against injustices towards minorities also took place because of the help that Facebook and other platforms offer to create vents and invite attendees. Social media has helped spread the awareness of Black Lives Matter and its https://obamawhitehouse.archives.gov/the-press-office/2013/07/19/remarks-president-trayvon-martin 4 message promoting peaceful coexistence within a multicultural society and ways to protest against any discrimination.

How Social Media can Undermine Peace by Promoting Violence

Despite mass media's attacks on the negative aspects of social media, as the above part of the essay explains, this is not always the case. Unfortunately, there are many reasons to be critical of how social media affects society as a whole. The negative effects on the mental health of the users of social media have been widely reported, but the dangers of how social media can be weaponised to bring about societal destabilisation are far worse. As mentioned above in the article, numerous extremist and terrorist groups have used different platforms as a means to promote their radical views and invite others to join their ranks. A very prime example of such activities would be that of the Islamic State of Iraq and Syria (ISIS).

ISIS and the Use of Social Media

The Islamic State of Syria and Iraq is a jihadist, fundamentalist Sunni Muslim terrorist group that was first a part of another notorious Muslim terror organisation—the al Qaeda—until it broke away. Apart from being a group, ISIS also formed its own "state" that encompassed large portions of Iraq and Syria, as well as a territory in Libya. Its goal was to establish a worldwide caliphate—a state that strictly follows the rules of the Islamic holy book, the Qur'an, and Sharia law—the laws of all aspects of life that have their roots in the Qur'an. To this end, ISIS has conducted a violent, terror-filled campaign to achieve this goal, with their activities going beyond the borders of the Middle East. Terrorist attacks have happened in Europe, Southeast Asia and Africa, and recruits came from countries like the United States and other democratic, secular nations. What made the people come to join such a vile organisation. One possible answer lies in the use of social media that was utilised by ISIS. Over the past two years, a large amount of media attention has been received with their effective usage of social networking to promote their message and attract new members. The strategic usage of social media by ISIS shows the resourcefulness of the movement, which has attracted an unprecedented 40,000 foreign nationals from 110 countries to enter its ranks. https://snap.stanford.edu/mis2/files/MIS2_paper_23.pdf 5 Increasing internet usage in Africa and the Middle East indicates that ISIS was able to strike fertile ground in terms of a population that could be manipulated to support them. Accounts of members of ISIS or pages that are directly owned by the group released propaganda piece, one after another, that purposefully showed that the group is much more affluent, powerful and resourceful than it really is. By appealing to prevalent Muslim norms in the region (albeit in a much more radical form), as well as giving misguided, troubled teens a false promise of glory, their ranks became bigger. Methods used also included the "hijacking" of popular trends in social media, i.e.: hashtags on Twitter/ Instagram to spread their content. Fortunately for most of us, people were able to see through this as nothing more than a pathetic attempt to appeal to the masses and report their posts. It goes without saying that the major networking companies took severe measures to find, remove and report to the authorities, ISIS-related content and users, in the hope of having these people apprehended (if possible), or at the least to prevent the spread of such propaganda. Despite such measures, the terrorist group caused much instability. From the ongoing wars in the Middle East to the wave of terrorist attacks in Western Europe, the Islamic State caused death and instability to large parts of the world. Fortunately, with the defeat of their "state" in Syria and Iraq, hopefully their capability to use social media for nefarious means will be reduced to zero. What if the use of social media could cause disruption to peace and security, but it didn't have to involve mass-scale death and terror? What if it could be used to divide people within one country through, let's say, political lines? This is exactly what happened in the 2016 US presidential election.

How Social Media Turned the 2016 US Presidential Election into a Toxic Event

During any election process since the advent of the Internet and social media, people tend to rally around their preferred candidate(s)/political party(ies) and show their support online. Discussions in comment sections or forums often tended to get heated and uncivilised, but this is a common occurrence and it doesn't disrupt nations. The 2016 election was different. You had two sides that were already on bad terms for years: the conservative Republican Party and the liberal Democratic Party. Before the general election, there was already frequent infighting between establishment Republicans (like Jeb Bush, Marco Rubio, John Kasich) and the controversial outsider Donald Trump, and the Democratic camp saw a sharp rivalry between democratic socialist Bernie Sanders and the centrist Hillary Clinton. But it was Donald Trump and Hillary Clinton who really set off the reaction that spurred social media into frenzy, ultimately causing divisions all around. Both candidates were disliked by the general population: Donald Trump was perceived as being xenophobic and vulgar, whereas Hillary Clinton as untrustworthy, secretive and elitist. Still, both candidates had a base of supporters that also utilised available platforms to prop up support. What set this election cycle apart; however, was how divisive it was. Trump and Clinton had their own accounts on social media, and used them to bypass the media and directly communicate with their base of support. Often times, the candidates clashed online between themselves, oftentimes not refraining from insults and this caused their supporters to take the insults outside of the World Wide Web. This resulted in violent protests at rallies, fights between supporters of each candidate, and the emergence of the alt right movement - a radical right wing ideology, focused on anti-immigration, a distrust for the establishment, and covert anti-Semitism. Another thing made matters worse—the use of bots. Bots are fake accounts run by AI (Artificial Intelligence) that operate like humans online. Bots post or exchange details that could be either that of praise or derogatory in tone towards a particular political nominee. The information posted by these bots illustrates the goal provided by other bot developers. The evidence they produce may be misleading and unrepresentative of the true beliefs of the populace. But what really made people mad were how the major tech companies shared the private information of its users for political means. Cambridge Analytica, a data mining and analysis company, used the data gathered in order to target the audience with sponsored content that reflected the views of these people. How did the company know these views? All the user had to do was like a page or link that had a politically-leaning content, and depending on its views (right wing/ conservative or left wing/liberal) and this was stored in Facebook's database and then handed over to Cambridge Analytica. This scandal raised serious questions of how private our accounts really are on the Internet. A certain phrase has emerged during this cycle that became prominent and widely used since then (possibly due to the usage by the winner of the 2016 presidential US election—Donald Trump). This phrase is "Fake news", and it has become the scorn of social media users and one if the major issues impacting it. https://www.e-ir.info/2017/07/28/social-media-in-the-2016-u-s-presidential-election/ 6

Fake News and how it Shapes Social Media and the World at Large

In short, fake news is any material that contains fraudulent, untrue information while posing itself as a legitimate source of news. This phenomenon has been as long as humans have been able to share news, often to mislead their perceived enemies, or as a means to manipulate their own people. The goals haven't changed, but access to fake news has never been easier, thanks to the Internet. Add to that a general mistrust of traditional media, and you get a population of people who don't recognise real news from fake and are willing to believe whatever they read on the internet. Some bits of information are meant to be harmless; even to be treated as a hoax. Unfortunately, some have lead to situations in which people's lives are at risk. For example, Dylan Roof, a young white man arrested for killing 12 Afro-American people in a Methodist Church, has read fake news about how black people rape white women at a higher rate and that a black person shoots and kills a white man every day. This caused him to radicalise to such a degree that he killed 12 innocent church goers, simply because they were black. But this is one example out of many in the world. These fake news have the capacity to polarise societies to such a degree that people can be ready to kill others simply because of something they read online. Fortunately, governments are beginning to realise that fake news is something that needs to be vigorously combated. Many federal departments are already putting up information to refute news programs that they find to be faked. We are still discussing and enforcing restrictions and banning outlets that report disinformation.

Conclusion

There is no one single conclusion that can be drawn about how social media can influence peace and security. As the essay presented, there are cases that serve a good purpose, and those that have only one goal - to spread division among peoples. Add to the fact that more and more people readily can access the Internet. Data held on mobile phones, computers and social network pages will reveal important and highly private details rendering individuals and organisations vulnerable to a variety of hostile forces (criminals, jihadists and authoritarian regimes). The core pillar of the new global, peaceful democracy is maintaining a compromise https://www.trendmicro.com/vinfo/pl/security/news/cybercrime-and-digital-threats/fake-news-cyber-7 propaganda the-abuse-of-social-media https://www.youth4peace.info/system/files/2018-04/2.%20TP_Social%20Media_SecDev.pdf, between collective stability and defence, democratic citizenship and the preservation of individual rights. Social media also serves a purpose in this; it can be used to further the cause of a peaceful coexistence between nations and groups of the world, as shown in the essay. Simultaneously, however, we cannot forget about the dangers that come along with social media. It is not only within the interest of the companies to combat divisive rhetoric, it is a citizen's duty to take notice of such hate-filled content whenever it appears online. There is no knowing of how social media will evolve, as it can change unexpectedly day to day. But the impact it has on peace and security will be there, and it will continue to grow as technologies become more available. There is a thin line between having a positive impact and doing harm online - what one perceives as fighting and pushing for justice online can be seen as a breach of personal freedoms to others. Ultimately, it lies within the global populace's hands to tread that thin line and decide how social media - a powerful tool in its own right - can be used to change the world.

REFERENCES

1. http://ddss.unipune.ac.in/images/logo/ _02082019_ 120801_02082019_ 115635 Concept%20Note%207-8%20,%202018%20%20co nf%20%20update.pdf
2. Reitere, Sarma. 2020. What social media Platforms Are Doing to Help During the Coronavirus, Socialbakers, Unified social media Marketing Platform. Accessed at https://www.socialbakers.com/blog/social-media-platforms-during-coronavirus on 5 April 2020.
3. Brown, Heather, Guskin, Emily and Mitchell, Amy. 2012. The Role of social media in the Arab Uprisings, Pew Research Centre. Accessed at https://www.journalism.org/2012/11/28/role-social-media-arab-uprisings/ on 14 February 2019.
4. Accessed at https://obamawhitehouse.archives.gov/the-press-office/2013/07/19/remarks-president-trayvonmartin on 9 February 2019.
5. Alfifi, Majid, Kaghazgaran Parisa, and Caverlee, James. 2018. Measuring the Impact of ISIS social media Strategy. Accessed at https://snap.stanford.edu/mis2/files/MIS2_paper_23.pdf on 11 January 2019.
6. Ellis, Matthew. 2017. Social media in the 2016 U.S. Presidential Election, E-International Relations. Accessed at https://www.e-ir.info/2017/07/28/social-media-in-the-2016-u-s-presidential-election/ on 8 February 2019.
7. Accessed at https://www.trendmicro.com/vinfo/pl/security/news/cybercrime-and-digital-threats/ fake-news-cyber-propaganda-the-abuse-of-social-media on 25 February 2019.
8. Accessed at https://www.youth4peace.info/system/files/ 2018-04/2.%20TP_Social%20Media_SecDev.pdf on 21 February 2019.

7

Impact of Social Media on Social Behaviour

Dr. Sushama Bhosale

Introduction

Social Media is becoming part of our society changing social norms and culture. Social media began in the form of generalized online communities. These online communities formed on websites like Geocities.com in 1994, Theglobe.com in 1995, and Tripod.com in 1995.[1] Many of these early communities focused on social interaction by bringing people together through the use of chat rooms. The chat rooms encouraged users to share personal information, ideas, or even personal web pages. Later the social networking community Classmates took a different approach by simply having people link to each other by using their personal email addresses. By the late 1990s, social networking websites began to develop more advanced features to help users find and manage friends.[2] These newer generation of social networking websites began to flourish with the emergence of Six Degrees.com in 1997, Make out club in 2000, Hub Culture in 2002, and Friendster in 2002.[3] However, the first profitable mass social networking website was the South Korean service, Cyworld.[4] Cyworld initially launched as a blog-based website in 1999 and social networking features were added to the website in 2001. Other social networking websites emerged like

Myspace in 2002, LinkedIn in 2003, and Bebo in 2005. In 2009, the social networking website Facebook (launched in 2004) became the largest social networking website in the world.[5] Active users of Facebook increased from just a million in 2004 to over 750 million by the year 2011. Making internet-based social networking both a cultural and financial phenomenon. A social network is a social structure made up of individuals or organizations who communicate and interact with each other. Social networking sites—such as Facebook, Twitter, and LinkedIn—are defined as technology-enabled tools that assist users with creating and maintaining their relationships. A study found that middle schooler's reported using social media to see what their friends are doing, to post pictures, and to connect with friends.[6] Human behaviour related to social networking is influenced by major individual differences.[7] Meaning that people differ quite systematically in the quantity and quality of their social relationships.[8] Two of the main personality traits that are responsible for this variability are the traits of extraversion and introversion.[9] Extraversion refers to the tendency to be socially dominant, exert leadership, and influence on others.[10] Contrastingly, introversion refers to the tendency of a person to have a disposition of shyness, social phobia, or even avoid social situations altogether, which could lead to a reduction in the number of potential contacts that person may have.[11] These individual differences may result in different social networking outcomes.[12] Other psychological factors related to social media are: depression, anxiety, attachment, self-identity, and the need to belong.

The usage of social media by youths has become a way of life and personal activities are made republic.[13] Many studies have been carried out on student usages of social media, its impact on their social behaviour, education, academic performance as well as the positive and negative impact. Khan (2012) conducted a research which focused on social media website on students.[12] While Ahn (2015) conducted a research on effect of social media on academic advancement and social well-being of adolescents.[13] If we utilized social media wisely it's a very good technology and tool for collaborative learning for students. Social media is giving platform to the students to participate in social discussions, posting comments, pictures, images, share ideas and many more as it influences youth daily life path and social interactions that influence overall social behaviour of students. Usage of social media may affect the feelings and emotions and could cause pain, hurt, mental and emotional breakdowns.[14] Gross (2004) stated that (a) the prediction of social media use by gender as boys appear to spend most of their time browsing the internet and playing games and girls engage in chatting; (b) use of social media leads to adolescent depression and isolation.[15] Growth and improvement of social media technology, research has proven that social media plays huge roles in the economy growth while it consequences includes: terrorist attack, cyber bullying, poaching for sexual exploitation and time wasting.[16]

Social media has created alternative new world of information, communication and interconnectivity order which cannot be activated using face-to-face method among students.[17] The new world order has reshaped and redefined student's social behaviour and social well-being. The use of social media in to the education at a large is attributed to its user-oriented features, and motivated tutors, students, education institutions to improve their interactions and teaching-learning delivery techniques. Students use social media for various reasons like communicating with friends, access to learning contents and sharing, group discussion forums, chat room, fun, game sharing and many more. Researchers showed that the usage of social media among students can bring positive and negative impacts. This social media can be addictive, time consuming, distractive, social gathering isolation, monophobia and many others. Usage of social media results in bad handwriting and spelling, lateness of class and assignment submission, addiction, few study time. These negative effects can be visualized on social behaviour and social lifestyle or cultural belief changes.

Method

Both primary and secondary data sources are used. The primary data is collected through personal data sheet and questionnaire on social media and secondary data was collected through using literature study. Aim of this study was to assess the impact of social media on social behaviour and lifestyle of university students. Using random sampling method total 155 university student, 79 male students and 76 female students of various postgraduate departments of Savitribai Phule Pune was selected for this study. Based on following main research questions the data was collected.

1. What are the perceptions of students on social media impact on their social behaviour?
2. What are the impacts of social media on social behaviour and social lifestyle of the students?
3. What are the positive and negative impacts of social media?

These questions are constructed with sub questions and the answers were given on 5-point scale, i.e. Strongly Agree, Agree, Disagree, Strongly Disagree, and Undecided.

A descriptive statistics method was used in understanding and exploring the effects of social media on social behaviour and lifestyle.

Analysis of Data

The use of social media has a great deal of impact on the user's behaviour. Analysis of basic information about use of preferred social media by both boys and girl students is shown in Table 1. Finding indicates that 100 per cent university students both boys and girls are using WhatsApp, 90.72 per cent boys and 93.72 per cent girls use Facebook 71.28 per cent boys and 59.4 per cent girls use Instagram, almost 57 per cent students (both boys and girls) use YouTube and the list continues.

Table1: Preferred Social Media Used by Students (N=155)

		Responses (N=155)			
		Boys (N=79)	*%*	*Girls (N=76)*	*%*
Preferred Social Media used by students	WhatsApp	79	100	76	100
	Facebook	72	90.72	71	93.72
	Instagram	54	71.28	45	59.40
	YouTube	46	57.96	43	56.76
	Twitter	38	47.88	16	21.12
	Skype	21	26.46	18	23.76

Analysis of Research Questions

Q1. What are the perceptions of students on social media impact on their social behaviour and social lifestyle?

Table 2: Perceptions of Students on Social Media impact on their Social Behaviour

No.	*Construct*	*SA*		*A*		*D*		*SD*		*UD*	
		M	*F*	*M*	*F*	*M*	*F*	*M*	*F*	*M*	*F*
1.	Social media is good tool for learning	35 44.45%	30 39.6%	22 27.94%	23 30.36%	9 11.43%	7 9.24%	9 11.43%	10 13.2	4 3.81%	6 7.92
2.	Social media is necessary for daily routine	36 45.72%	32 42.10%	23 29.21%	21 27.72%	8 10.16%	9 11.88	8 10.16%	11 14.52%	4 3.81%	3 3.96
3.	Social media is helpful to getting knowledge	32 40.64%	36 47.52%	22 27.94%	24 31.68%	8 10.16%	4 5.28%	9 11.43%	4 5.28%	8 10.16%	8 10.56%
4.	Social media is time consuming	32 40.64%	36 47.52%	30 38.1%	29 38.28	5 6.35%	5 6.6%	4 3.81%	4 5.28%	8 10.16%	2 2.64%
5.	Social media affects negatively on personal relationship and family	35 44.45%	35 46.2%	25 31.75%	29 38.28	6 7.62%	4 5.28	4 3.81%	5 6.6%	9 11.43%	3 3.96%

Analysis of Table 2 is focused on the answers given on five-point scale. However, undecided students' results were not considered in the further analysis because their opinions are not matched with the agree or disagree category. Table 2 indicates that more than 60 per cent boys and girls agree that social media is good tool for learning and necessary for daily routine. However, at the same time more than 60 per cent boys and girls agree that social media is time consuming and it affects negatively on personal relationships and family.

Q2.What are the impacts of social media on social behaviour and social lifestyle of the students?

Analysis of Table 3 is focused on the answers given on five-point scale. Social media usage promotes good social norms to which 45.72 per cent male students and 42.10 per cent by female students agree with as well as agreed by 29.21 per cent male students and 27.72 per cent by female students. Participants also strongly agreed that social media impacts lifestyle of the students as well as Use of social media encourages to disregard the marriage institution in the society. But impact of the posting of irrelevant racist, abusive, anti-cultural and religious contents and links promote hatred among racial groups in the society was strongly disagreed with by 38.1 per cent male students and 38.28 per cent female students and surprisingly undecided by 40.64 per cent male students and 47.52 per cent female students.

Table 3: Impact of Social Media on Social Behaviour and Social Lifestyle of the Students

No.	*Construct*	*SA*		*A*		*D*		*SD*		*UD*	
		M	*F*	*M*	*F*	*M*	*F*	*M*	*F*	*M*	*F*
1.	Social media usage promotes good social norms	36 45.72%	32 42.10%	23 29.21%	21 27.72%	8 10.16%	9 11.88%	8 10.16%	11 14.52%	4 3.81%	3 3.96%
2.	Posting of irrelevant racist abusive anticultural and religious contents and links promotes hatred among racial groups in the society	8 10.16%	2 2.64%	4 3.81%	4 5.28%	5 6.35%	5 6.60%	30 38.1%	29 38.28%	32 40.64%	36 47.52%
3.	Use of social media encourages to disvalue the marriage institution in the society	35 44.35%	35 46.2%	25 31.75%	29 38.28%	5 7.62%	5 5.28%	8 10.16%	2 2.64%	4 5.28%	4 3.81%
4.	Use of social media impacts on lifestyle of the students	32 40.64%	36 47.52%	30 38.1%	29 38.28	5 6.35%	5 6.6%	4 3.81%	4 5.28%	8 10.16%	2 2.64%

Q3. What are the positive and negative impacts of social media?

No.	*Construct*	*SA*		*A*		*D*		*SD*		*UD*	
		M	*F*	*M*	*F*	*M*	*F*	*M*	*F*	*M*	*F*
1.	Promotes borrowing foreign culture	38 48.10%	36 47.36%	26 32.91%	28 36.84%	3 3.79%	5 6.57%	5 7.62%	3 3.79%	7 8.86%	4 3.81%
2.	Helps destroying gender inequality	35 44.35%	35 46.2%	25 31.75%	29 38.28%	5 6.32%	5 6.57%	8 10.16%	2 2.64%	4 5.28%	4 3.81%
3.	Encourages for extra-marital relationships	41 51.89%	39 51.48%	21 26.67%	23 30.36%	9 11.43%	8 10.56%	7 8.89%	6 7.92%	- -	- -
4	Destroys emotional and mental health	32 40.64%	36 47.52%	30 38.1%	29 38.28	5 6.35%	5 6.6%	4 3.81%	4 5.28%	8 10.16%	2 2.64%
5	Addiction	36 45.72%	32 42.10%	23 29.21%	21 27.72%	8 10.16%	9 11.88%	8 10.16%	11 14.52%	4 3.81%	3 3.96%

Analysis of Table 3 is focused on the answers given on five-point scale on the positive and negative aspects of social media. As showed in

Table 3, social media helps to promote foreign culture is strongly agreed with by 48.10 per cent male students and 47.36 per cent of female students. More than 44 per cent male students and 46 per cent female students agreed that social media helps to destroy gender inequality. Social media encourages extra-marital relationships is strongly agreed with by almost 52 per cent male students and female students. And no undecided status was shown for this construct. Social media is a strong addiction was strongly agreed with by 45.72 per cent of male students and 42.10 per cent of female students.

Discussion

social media creates a better channel for connectivity, communication, discussion and interaction between people in global era. Data analysis of this study focused on getting constructive information on perceptions of students on social media impact on their social behaviour as well as on their lifestyle and the other positive and negative impacts of the use of social media. This study found that more than 80 per cent of the male and female students suggest that social media impacted their social behaviour and lifestyle.

This study reported that more than 80 per cent participants strongly agreed that social media promotes 21st century education and teaching learning pedagogy. These findings were supported by Chen et. al.

This study agrees with the Ahn, J. (2015). Al-Sharq et. al. (2015) research findings supported this study indicating that social media has brought change in social norm and it is helping to borrow the social foreign culture. The findings of this research showed that all the participants do not agree orare undecided about the construct of posting of irrelevant racist abusive anti-cultural and religious contents and links, promotes hatred among racial groups in the society while using social media. The study also found that use of social media is addiction. Social media encourages extra-marital relationships is strongly agreed with by almost 52 per cent male students and female students.

This study showed that use of social media affects on perception, social behaviour and lifestyle of youth. It was able to discover diverse impacts of social media usages both positive and negative which are a result of advancement in modern technology.

REFERENCES

1. Cotriss, David (2008). Where are they now: The Globe. Com, The Industry Standard. Accessed at http://www.thestandard.com/news/2008/05/29/ where-are-they-now-theglobe-com on 8 January 2019.
2. Romm-Livermore, C. & Setzekorn, K. (2008). Social Networking Communities and E-Dating Services: Concepts and Implications, USA: Information Science Reference (IGI Global), p. 271.
3. Gibby Miller (2008). "Inventing the Social Network", Accessed at https://www.cbsnews.com/news/gibby-miller-inventing-the-social-network/ on 30 December 2018.
4. Thelwall, M. & Stuart, D. (2010). Social Network Sites. In Panayiotis Zaphiris & Chee Siang Ang, Social Computing and Virtual Communities, p. 271.
5. Kazeniac, Andy (2009). "Social Networks: Facebook Takes Over Top Spot, Twitter Climbs". Accessed at Blog.compete.com on 7August 2013.
6. Kim, Jeong-a; Namgung, Jeeyeong (2018). "Identifying Latent Classes of Educational Outcomes of Middle School Students and Testing Determinants of the Classes". Korean Educational Research Association. 56 (1), pp. 219–44.
7. Thompson, E. R. (2008). "Development and Validation of an International English Big-Five Mini-Markers". Personality and Individual Differences. 45 (6), pp. 542–48.
8. Chamorro-Premuzic, T.; Bennett, E.; Furnham, A. (2007). "The happy personality: Mediational role of trait emotional intelligence". *Personality and Individual Differences*. 42 (8), pp. 1633–39.
9. Steele, R. S.; Kelly, T. J. (1976). "Eysenck Personality Questionnaire and Jungian Myers-Briggs type indicator correlation of extraversion-introversion". *Journal of Consulting and Clinical Psychology*. 44 (4), p. 690.
10. Lu, H. P.; Hsiao, K. L. (2010). "The influence of extro/introversion on the intention to pay for social networking sites". *Information & Management*, 47 (3), pp. 150–57.
11. Edge Windon. (2017). Nursing Professionalism: Impact of social media Use among Nursing Students, Accessed at https://www.researchgate.net/publication/318497510_Nursing_Professionalism_Impact_of_Social_Media_Use_among_Nursing_Students on 20 December 2018.
12. Edge, Windon (2017), "Impact of social media Use among Nursing Students". *Journal of Healthcare Communications*, 2(3). Accessed at https://healthcare-communications.imedpub.com/nursing-professionalism-impact-of-social-media-use-among-nursing-students.php?aid=19283 on 23 January 2019.
13. Khan, Shahzad (2012). "Impact of social networking websites on students", *Abasyn Journal of Social Sciences*, 5(2), pp. 56–77.
14. Ahn, J. (2011). "The effect of social network sites on adolescents' social and academic development: Current theories and controversies", *Journal of the Association for Information Science and Technology*, 62(8), pp. 1435–45.
15. Lowisz, Steve. (2014). "The Influence of social media on Today's Culture". Accessed at stevelowisz.com/wp.../02/The-Influence-of-Social-media-in-Todays-Culture-wp.pdf on 18 January 2019.
16. Wolf, D. M, Wenskovitch, J & Anton, B. B (2016)," Use of Internet and Social Media: Does age, years of experience and educational level make a difference?". *Journal of*

Nursing Education and Practice, 6(2), pp. 68–75.

17. Makinde, O. A, Odimegwu. C. O, Abdulmlik, J. O, Babalola, S. O & Fawole, O. I. (2016). Gender-Based Violence following social media Acquaintance in Nigeria. *African Journal of Reproductive Health*, December Vol.20 (4), p. 67.
18. Chukwuere, J. E., & Onyebukwa, C. F. (2017 July). New media and politics: An assessment of 2016 South African local government elections. In Proceedings of International Academic Conferences (No.4607534). International Institute of Social and Economic Sciences.
19. Chen, C.C. Kaewkitipong L & Ractham. (2016). Using Social Media to enrich information systems field trip experience: Students satisfaction and continuance intentions. *Computers in Human Behaviour*, Vol. 63, pp. 256–63.
20. Al-Sharqi, L, Hashim, K & Kutbi, I. (2015).Perceptions of social media Impact on students social behaviour: Comparison between Arts and Science Students. *International Journal of Education and Social Science*, 2(4) pp. 122–31.
21. Junco, R. Helbergert, G & Loken. E. (2011).The effect of twitter on college student engagement and grades. *Journal of Computer Assisted Learning*, Vol. 27, pp.119–32.

8

The Implications of Social Media on National Security of India

Dr. A. Thennarasu

"War is too serious to be left to computers".

Introduction

We in the world face new kind of warfare not on the battlefield in the traditional sense, but in the various spheres of the social media, one can say. This takes us to revisit what Alvin Toffler has to say. According to Alvin Toffler, "The full implications of what we termed 'Third wave knowledge warfare' have not yet been digested. The wars of the future will increasingly be prevented, won or lost based on information superiority and dominance. Cyber-war involves everything from strategic deception and perception management down to tactical disruption of an adversary's information systems."[1]

Today, one can attract the world's attentions to your cause, case, action just with the help of social media thereby emphasizing cost effectiveness in one's attempt with ease. Information has always been important to human beings in all their endeavours. Throughout history, individuals, groups and nations have strived to expand the information available to them and restrict that available to the adversary or competitor. Knowledge and the information explosion resulting from the industrial revolution and the requirement of its dissemination to the people at large gave rise to what was termed 'information overload'. Research in the fields of Information and Communication Technology (ICT) enabled the storage of large amounts of information, fast processing, and retrieval.

Today, Information is power; we are now in the information society. Information and communication technology is the most effective instrument of social and political change influencing all segments of public, namely share holders, employees, customers, suppliers, general community, media public, etc. IT as new mass media offers ample opportunities for public relations to reach the target audience which has led to E-public relations. Infact, the new mass media: Internet, website,e-mail ushered in electronic public relations. As a result of IT technology, the conventional media such as newspapers, radio, film and television turned to be the old media and IT media such as the computer, Internet,e-mail,website became the new mass media.

These developments in the field of ICT brought about a paradigm change in the human capacity to handle information. Amongst other things, ICT brought about a quantum leap in efficiency in the core sectors of the economy like industry, communications, transportation, energy, etc. On the flip side, this increased efficiency made these sectors heavily dependent on the use of information and ICT. This dependence, in turn, increased the vulnerability of the core sectors, and the society at large, to disruption in the flow of information. Information as an entity and its flow are more vulnerable and need to be protected like other national assets. Long recognised as one of the elements of national power, along with diplomacy, military and economic power, information has assumed greater weightage in the present society. This phenomenal rise in the importance of information in the late 20th century led military thinkers to treat information both as a weapon and a target in modern conflicts.

War is routinely defined as news, while peace is not. The government response to the hijacking of the passenger flight IC-814 to Kandahar, which in no case can be called an ideal decision, was largely influenced by the media. Similarly, the media's reporting of Army units and formation, movements in accurate detail suggests the insensitivity to the national security matters. In the wake of Indian parliamentary attack by Pakistani elements, India mobilized army along the western border. The media was doing the job of reporting India's efforts to mobilize and its strategic formation moves. Nothing could be more damaging to Indian national security under such circumstances.

The Indian Media's Kargil episode had darker side as well Post-Kargil, on July 29, 1999, the union government appointed a committee under the chairmanship of Shri K. Subrahmanyam to review and recommend measures related to Kargil. The report stated, "All things considered, coverage by the print and electronic media was by large satisfactory, Yet it was apparent that with some exceptions, media personnel lacked training in military affairs and war reporting and the Armed services lacked training and preparedness to facilitate the task of the media and counter disinformation". The manner in which anti-terror operations by security agencies is covered is one of the most important issues with regard to responsibility of media in contemporary times. Intelligence agencies had claimed the real-time coverage of the 26/11 terror attack in Mumbai had helped the handlers of terrorists holed up in the Taj and Oberoi hotels to get information about what the security agencies were doing. During the limited duration when the security operation is on, a very strict discipline on the kind of reporting will have to be maintained.

Freedom of speech and expression is a complex right. Firstly, because it is not an absolute right, it may be restricted to protect other overriding public interests(such as national security and private interests (such as a person 's right to privacy). Secondly, it protects both right of the speaker and right to listener, in the latter case to receive a diversity of information and ideas. Sometimes these rights appear to come into conflict. Consequently, allocating priority between them can require a difficult balancing exercise. In fact, the ultimate goal for regulating media should be to protect and deepen the fundamental rights, including the right to speech and expression.

Although these Norms provide for a number of guidelines, not all of them are followed by the media on most occasions, for example the norms provide that particulars relating to the identity of rape victims should not be revealed by the media. However, in the gang rape case now popularly referred to as the "Nirbhaya Rape" case, the media revealed a large amount of personal details of the victim, which is more than enough for any person acquainted with the women in the present or future to identify them. It is clearly a violation of the norms of journalistic conduct as well as the intent of the laws protecting the identity of rape victims.

Traditionally the Press Council Act has only regulated offline media, but in 2012 the PCI publicly announced the need to amend the Press council act to include electronic media so that such forms of media are to be brought within the scope of the PCI or a similar regulatory body. Citing the incident of a viral SMS threat to individuals from the North East in Bangalore, which resulted in a mass exodus from the city in mid-2012, the PCI recognized that the unregulated electronic media is playing havoc with the lives of the people.

The Act empowers the government to prohibit the operation of any cable television network in such areas as are notified in the official gazette, and restrict the transmission of any channel it thinks is necessary or expedient to do so in the interest of the sovereignty or integrity of India, security of India, friendly relations of India with any foreign states or for decency, morality or public order which are also found in various other legislations (such as Telegraph Act, Information Technology Act, etc.) this Act also adds ground such as decency or morality for actions.

Cyber Warfare in the Military Domain

In the military domain, operations that are undertaken to gain information superiority fall under the ambit of 'Information Warfare' (IW). Within that ambit, offensive and defensive 'Information Operations' (IO) are waged by means of weaponised intervention, electronic warfare etc., 'cyber warfare' being one such mean that is prosecuted in the cyber-space. Cyber warfare therefore is truly a 'military operations of war', to be conducted as an element of offensive and defensive IO, and waged in the same spirit of ultimate measures. It is distinguished by predominance of offensive content and is to be prosecuted through military-dedicated IT-based satellites, data warehouses, maps, communication networks, GPS, UAV, AWACs, PGM, etc. However, while civil functions are to be operational at all times, the military function during peace-time is to prepare and test continuously, letting go at war-time to disable the opponent's military, quasi-military and civil infrastructure. Herein lies the distinction between the civil and military functions of cyber security. Conversely, there are many commonalities between the two functions with respect to the above discussed civil cyber security mechanisms as well as the software skills, hardware and processes.

Advantages of Using Social Media

The following are the advantages why certain groups choose social media to attack India as safe haven.

(1) Command and Control Warfare (C2W): The objective is to attack the adversary's ability to generate and communicate commands to its forces and disable or corrupt his Defence Information Infrastructure (DII).

(2) Intelligence Based Warfare (IBW): It is the integration of sensors, processors and data-links to achieve efficient reconnaissance, surveillance, target acquisition, target engagement and finally, damage assessment.

(3) Electronic Warfare (EW): Communication as well as non-communication combat to achieve degradation, disorientation, interruption and corruption of the adversary's electro-magnetic emissions is classified as EW. In other words, it implies domination of electro-magnetic spectrum.

(4) Psychological Warfare: This is aimed at targeting the adversary's mental orientation and perception, and thereby influences his intent.

(5) Hacker Warfare: This is defined as destruction, degradation or corruption of adversary's computer data-base and automated decision support and executive processes.

(6) Infrastructural Warfare: Under the civil functions, this involves 'information blockade' and 'information imperialism' to derive political and economic advantage. Under warlike conditions, its extreme manifestation leads to attacks on the adversary's primary infrastructure – railways, power plants, oil sector etc.

Social Media and the Indian Context

Even though the Indian armed forces are capable of protecting physical borders, in today's Information Age, movement of ideas, information and knowledge needs to be regulated more than the physical movement of people. The Information Age has thrown up many new challenges that need to be addressed in order to maintain India's position as a leading nation in the world community. In the past, because of our weak patent laws and non-codification of traditional knowledge, many ideas and concepts were lost to the so-called developed nations that were quick to patent them in their own countries. Even the ubiquitous Neem has several properties and chemicals that have been patented abroad for their efficacy against various bacteria or as an antibiotic, etc. Information exfiltration through computer hacking has emerged amongst the most serious threats to information security. Computer network attacks that have been traced to China have targeted India's core sectors, including the Information Technology (IT) sector, in one instance even taking away a lucrative contract from a third country. China has even tried to penetrate various Indian government servers, including those at the National Security Adviser's (NAS) office. One such attempt on December 15, 2010, was admitted by our former National Security Advisor Mr. M.K. Narayanan when he said, "This was not the first instance to hack into our computers." The attack came in the form of an e-mail with a PDF attachment containing a Trojan which allows a hacker to access a computer remotely and download or delete files. The first step towards the development of the Indian information warfare concept, therefore, would be to define India's priorities and national interests in the information sphere. The information sphere would include all available information in both civil and military arenas, and accumulated knowledge whether in electronic, print or any other media or traditional knowledge passed down by word of mouth or execution methodologies unique to a particular area or community, etc.

It also touches upon the cultural and spiritual lives of the people. Information security, for the purpose of defining IW can then be thought of as "the state of protection of India's national interests in the information sphere defined by the totality of interests of its citizens, including NRIs, society at large, and the (Indian) nation-state." The importance of information, during both peace and war, necessitates formulation of IW concepts for the entire spectrum of peace, operations other than war, imminence of hostilities and full-fledged war. Taking the necessity to include both offensive and defensive elements into consideration, a proposed Indian definition of IW could read like: Information Warfare is a form of competition between two or more sides, consisting of both nation-states and non-state actors, involving use of special means (informational, cyber, psychological or technical) and methods of influencing the other party's information resources, and also of protecting one's own information/knowledge resources, in order to achieve assigned goals and broader national interests.

Conclusion

Today, conflicts cannot remain localised but rapidly become internationalised. Every nation has to keep the global ramifications of any action against another nation in mind. With the global and instant reach of the media, and thanks to the all-pervasive technology, information warfare assumes great importance. Today, wars are not just fought on the battlefields but as much in the minds of the stakeholders. Wars are now increasingly network-centric.

The Indian Armed Forces have attained sufficient capability in this regard. With its increasing influence as an emerging superpower, India would do well to learn and practice the art of perception management not only in the diplomatic sphere but also in its doctrines of handling of information warfare. If we allow our enemies to use social media in a optimised way, then our armed forces morale and the values area at stake. In India however, we don't have a comprehensive national cyber security strategy to counter the cyber threats posed by our adversaries through social media which is the need of the hour. The serial bomb blasts in 2008 and even theIndian Parliament attack had the vestiges of the opponents using social media against us. It is advisable that we could have a separate wing in our armed forces to tackle such social media related attacks on our national security.

REFERENCES

1. Brig. Kapoor, B.M. (2009), The Art of Perception Management in Information Warfare Today, The United Service Institution of India, New Delhi. Accessed at https://usiofindia.org/publication/usi-journal/the-art-of-perception-management-in-information-warfare-today-2/#:~:text= According%20to%20Alvin%20 Toffler%2C%20%E2%80%9CThe,on%20information%20superiority%20and%20dominance. On 20 December 2018.

9

Globalization, Rise of New Media and the National Security

Dr. Biswajit Mohapatra

It is not strange that the Cold War and the design of the Web took place at exactly the same time.[1] This is particularly so after Marshall McLuhan, in his famous book, *Understanding Media: The Extensions of Man*,[2] had declared that "the medium is the message", pointing to a much too often ignored fact that media and technology themselves, exercise influence on human 2018, experience and understanding of the world and as such on our society as well. Since the 1980s media has undergone radical changes from being merely print and analog broadcast models (television and radio) to that of being now based upon new media technologies. In fact in the last thirty-five years, the old media has rapidly transformed into media, which is now predicated upon human use of digital technologies, e.g., Internet.

In the words of Andrew L. Shapiro, the "emergence of new, digital technologies signals a potentially radical shift of who is in control of information, experience and resources."[3] According to W. Russell Neuman, "the new media have technical capabilities to pull in one direction, while economic and social forces pull back in the opposite direction."[4] He further said, "We are witnessing the evolution of a universal interconnected network of audio, video, and electronic text communications that will blur the distinction between interpersonal and mass communication and between public and private communication".[5] He was farsighted enough to have laid bare the features of the new media, where he had pointed out its distinguishing features, *interalia*, (i) covering far geographic distance, (ii) allowing huge increase in the volume of communication, (iii) increasing the speed of communication, (iv) having opportunities for interactive communication and (v) enabling forms of communication which may overlap and interconnect. On the other hand, Lister et al.[6] have pointed out the positive and negative potential and actual implications of new media technologies, holding forth that the effects of media were hardly determined by the technology themselves and advised us to stay away from any notion of technological determinism. Nevertheless, the introduction of New Media, such as the internet, will reduce the amount of time individuals would spend on existing "Old" Media, which could ultimately lead to the end of such traditional media.[7]

The rise of new media as has enabled increased communication amongst people the world over facilitated by the Internet, it has also allowed people to rapidly express themselves through blogs, websites, videos, pictures, blogs etc. "As a result of the evolution of new media technologies, globalization occurs."[8] Globalization is understood as "more than expansion of activities beyond the boundaries of particular nation states".[9] In the words of Carely "By the enabling electronic communication, Globalization shortens the distance between people all over the world".[10] This new media "radically break the connection between physical place and social place, making physical location much less significant for our social relationships."[11] The changing new media environment tends to influence the "public sphere".[12] As per Ingrid Volkmer, "public sphere" as a process gets altered as the public communication "becomes restructured and partly disembedded from national political and cultural institutions."[13] "This trend of the globalized public sphere is not only as a geographical expansion forms a nation to worldwide, but also changes the relationship between the public, the media and state."[14] "Virtual communities" are established online and they transcend geographical boundaries, eliminating social restrictions.[15] Manovich and Castells have held that whereas mass media "corresponded to the logic of industrial mass society, which values conformity over individuality,"[16] new media follows the logic of the post-industrial or globalized society whereby "every citizen can construct her own custom lifestyle and select her ideology from a large number of choices".[17]

New Media: Characteristics and Functions

According to Martin Lister, et al,[18] new media has six main characteristics. The main characteristics include aspects as, (i) Digital, (ii) Interactivity, (iii) Hypertextual, (iv) Virtual, (v) Networked, and (vi) Simulated.

The new media as is everything Digital can be found as an output and as such its output form is seen in electronic formats, that generates, stores, processes data and is online sources, quite contrary to analogue data, which involved the process of storing physical properties in physical form. While analogue media is said to be fixed, since it does not change, the digital media is in a continuous state of flux. It is seen as constantly flowing, changing, besides improving.

This new media, due to its interactivity capability, allows consumers and users to get more involved, as a two-way form of communication. People are also able to make individualized lifestyle choices from out of the possibilities in the market. This interactivity besides engaging the user with media texts also enables a more independent relation to sources of knowledge, individualized media use, and greater choice.

Its other qualities, such as Hypertextual, Networked, Virtual (immersion and engagement in an environment constructed with computer graphics and digital video, letting users have control over their interaction) and Simulation (the creation of an artificial world that represents a real one), allowing predictions and visualizations over time makes it a very powerful medium.

It is well known that a media as the plural of medium, i.e. plurality of means of communication. Its major function is information, i.e. dissemination of information. As such this information, majority of which is disseminated by internet, or internet oriented media, can be, like old media, opinionated, objective, subjective, primary or even secondary.

This new media has the potential to provide information and education at the same time. In the developing countries, new media is used to spread mass awareness amongst the people, for eradication of social evils and superstitions, as has happened in case of Nepal. Besides providing for entertainment, it is also a source of infotainment and edutainment. Importantly it helps in the process of socialization, in the transmission of culture. It is said to be playing an immense role in disseminating the global culture, popularly known as internet culture. New media by enabling social networking, through Facebook and twitter, has socialized people, by linking them throughout the world, provides a common platform, where ideas, lifestyle reactions and behaviours are shared and influences people to behave in ways that are acceptable in today's culture or society, negotiated through websites, web archives, newsgroups, blogs and emails, etc.

As such it has been used as a tool for social change, in case of certain social movements. This new media can be seen to have been extensively used by these social movements for educating, organizing, communicating and building coalition amongst the masses. In 1994, the Zapatista Army of National Liberation of Chiapas, Mexico was the first, to effectively use the new media to organize the communiques, which made it a great successful movement. The WTO protests in 1999 used this internet media to organize, communicate and educate the rallyists which proved to be a great tool in the democratization of information, highlighting it to be another feature of new media. In the eyes of some scholars, the democratization is an indication of the creation of a "radical, socio-technical paradigm to challenge the dominant, neoliberal and technologically determinist model of information and communication technologies."[19]

New Media and Threats to National Security

As can be seen from above, the New social media also has the potential to be an important tool for the countries as well to promote their interest and values. But in the past ten years or so, it has been pointed out, that its peaceful evolution has eroded their own nation's system of values and also compromised national security. As the Internet and social media have constantly grown and been changing, steps to protect national security has not kept pace with times. In our so called modern times, social media has also emerged as a growing threat to our national security.

New Media changes continuously and is constantly modified and redefined due to its constant interaction with users, emerging technologies, cultural changes, etc. This New Media has been of great interest for global espionage, which is easily able to access the internet based electronic databases for collecting critical information. The national governments have also taken a great liking to the use of new media for reverse engineering for their own sake. It has become the medium for fast and certain collection of individuals' personal information by both private and government agencies. Its ready use for automatic creation of dossiers on both important people and the average citizen has raised the stakes of individual privacy and also spectre of data theft and manipulation, putting the individuals and the countries to a great risk.

Internet media as an interactive medium is rapidly growing due the possibility of its rapid dissemination from different internet access points, the digitalization of media, and media convergence. The new media based on communication technologies enables user-to-user interactivity and also interactivity between user and information.[20] The new media is a "many-to-much" web of communication, instead of the traditional mass communication media which was a "one-to-many" model. It has enabled individuals with access to appropriate technology, to produce his or her online media and include images, text, and sound about whatever he or she chooses.[21] This convergence of new methods of communication with new technologies is now radically reshaping the ways one interacts and communicates with one another. Another aspect is that the New Media changes continuously as it is constantly modified and redefined due to the close interaction between the users, emerging technologies and consequently change in our culture, etc. With social networks having become one of the fastest growing industries in the world and its enabling of building fast relationships among the users and closer communication through digital media and social networking sites, all of which have a unique characteristic and purpose, pose a variety of challenges to individual and nation's security as well. The two, digital media and social networking sites, seem to go hand-in-hand as far as increasing insecurity in the society is concerned but not in creating consistently valuable, relevant, and consistent content to attract and retain the clearly defined audience, i.e. the citizens, for national security.

According to N. Balakrishnan, "Social networking sites are a threat to national security as they are used as tools for drugs trafficking, money laundering etc".[22] Pointing to North East exodus from Bengaluru in 2012, he further said, 'these sites are also used to spark communal tensions, harm nation's social fabric, when false messages went viral with the use of fake IDs, taking advantage of the fact that automated machines can send thousands of tweets without human intervention."[23] With botnets, which are nothing but malicious softwares, being capable of controlling computers without the owners' knowledge, there is the possibility of it falling into nation's enemy's hands leading to data theft and its use for spreading hatred and erosion of nation's sovereignty. There are reports of inimical forces having taken to the use of social media for their narrow sectional interests and committing unspoken violence against the citizens.

With the rise in the use of internet media by the anti-national forces including the terrorists both within the national boundaries and across, to spread terror, it has become a common phenomenon to regulate social media and ban use of internet in times of civil disturbances. Many a time the government has felt the need to regulate social media, in stricter terms, urging the internet and telecom service providers to explore possible options for blocking mobile applications, including Facebook, WhatsApp, Instagram and Telegram, in situations where national security and public order are under threat.[24] Under Section 69A of the Information Technology Act,[25] the government of India has the power to block the applications". The law authorizes the central government or any officer authorized by it to issue direction to block information on the internet in the interest of sovereignty and integrity of India, defence of India, security of the state, friendly relations with foreign states or public order, or for preventing incitement to the commission of any cognizable offence relating to them".[26] But this move has been opposed by firms and individuals who are dedicated towards the cause of freedom of individuals and entities. They have urged the government to rather focus on implementation of laws on the ground instead of controlling internet. The telecom companies have also opposed the move. The

Director General of Cellular Operators Association of India, Rajan Mathews has said, "Trying to shutdown an application that is widely used may not be the best way to proceed".[27] In order to be able to counter false and targeted disinformation, that is being resorted to by vested interests, the government rather needs to improve governance within the country and establish close coordination with other national and international agencies to track down the miniscule population, who incite violence, disenfranchise the majority and disempower them and stop the malicious activities that the new media is being used for and enhance its national security.

REFERENCES

1. Manovich, Lev (2003), "New Media from Borges to HTML." *The New Media Reader.* Noah Wardrip-Fruin and Nick Montfort (eds), Massachusetts: Cambridge, pp.13–25.
2. McLuhan, Marshall (1964), Understanding Media: The Extensions of Man, Toronto: McGraw Hill.
3. Croteau, David and Hoynes, William (2003), Media Society: Industries, Images and Audiences (third edition), Thousand Oaks: Pine Forge Press, p. 303.
4. Ibid, p. 322.
5. Ibid.
6. Lister, Martin, Dovey, Jon, Giddins, Seth, Grant, Iain and Kelly, Kieran (2003) New Media: A Critical Introduction, London: Rutledge.
7. Dimmick, J., Chen, Y., and Li, Z. (2004). Competition between the Internet and Traditional News Media: The gratification-opportunities niche dimension, *Journal of Media Economics*, 17(1), pp. 19–33.
8. Flew, Terry (2002), *New Media: An Introduction*, UK: Oxford University Press, p. 13.
9. Thompson, John B. (1995). *The Media and Modernity*. Cambridge: Polity Press, p. 150.
10. Flew, op.cit.
11. Croteau and Hoynes, op.cit. p. 311.
12. Violaine Hacker, "Building Media's industry while promoting community of values in the globalisation", Politické Vedy, *Journal of International Affairs, Policy and Security*, 2/2011, http://www.fpvmv.umb.sk/politickevedy
13. Volkmer, Ingrid (1999) News in the Global Sphere. A Study of CNN and its impact on Global Communication, Luton: University of Luton Press, p.123.
14. Ibid.
15. DeFleur, Everette E. Dennis, Melvin L. (2010).*Understanding media in the digital age: connections for communication, society, and culture*. New York: Allyn & Bacon.
16. Manovich, Lev (2001) *The Language of New Media*, Cambridge and London: MIT Press.
17. Ibid.
18. Lister, et. al., op.cit.

19. Preston, Paschal (2001), "Reshaping Communications: Technology, Information and Social Change," London: Sage.
20. Schorr, Angela, Schenk, Michael and Campbell, William (2003), *Communication Research and Media Science in Europe*, Berlin: De Gruyter Mouton, p. 57.
21. Op.cit., Croteau, David & Hoynes, William, p. 303.
22. *The Times of India*, December 7, 2013, accessed at http://timesofindia.indiatimes.com/articleshow/26983917.cms?utm_source= contentofinterest&utm_medium=text&utm_campaign=cppst, on 2 March 2019.
23. Ibid.
24. Government Exploring Options to Block social media Apps, accessed at, https://www.ndtv.com/india-news/government-exploring-options-to-block-social-media-apps-activists-oppose-1896894, on 2 March 2019.
25. The Information Technology Act, 2008. Accessed at https://police.py.gov.in/Information%20Technology%20Act%202000%20-%202008%20(amendment).pdf on 10 December 2018.
26. Ibid.
27. Op. cit., 24.

10

Impact of Social Media on Security

Dr. M.L. Sali

Introduction

The term security is a comprehensive phenomenon and every factor of a country has a great relevance with it. But when we talk about security in a wider context then it becomes National Security. The basic meaning of National Security is an ability of a Nation to protect the internal values from external aggression. National security encompasses internal and external security along-with socio-cultural, political, economic, and strategic dimensions.[1] Owing to revolutionary and evolutionary changes in Science and Technology, "Society" has been subject of long term implications in every respect. Since the advent of industrial, then information and technologyrevolutions, drastic changes have occurred, problem of security became complicated. So the aim of this chapter is to highlight how social media has relevance to "Security" in wider context. In order to study the linkages between National Security and Social Media an analytical approach has been adopted.

Meaning and Concept of Social Media

Media means the means of mass communication broadcasting publishing and the internet regarded collectively. There are tentatively three types of media, i.e. Press, Electronic Media and nowadays social media. It is blamed that press had a negative role in escalating the tension during the pre and post-World War-I era,[2] whereas electronic media has been playing a very crucial role since 1945 onwards. By virtue of mobile, laptop, computer, internet, etc., the new media came into existence which is recognized as social media. Through this "Social Media," anyone can be online as empowered by an unrestricted flow of informations to be accumulated with their knowledge bank.[3]

Social media is a means of interacting with the people where they can create, share and exchange information and ideas in virtual communities and networks. In view of the meaning of social media, it is definedas, 'social media is the collective of online communications channels dedicated to community-based input, interaction, contact sharing and collaboration.'[4]

The revolution of information and technology has introduced new ways, means and methods of social communication. The emergence of new kind of media which became very popular and came to be known as "Social Media" has changed methods of socialization and interaction. This social media created thousands of friends which are virtual only. In view of this fact the social relationship seems to be virtual than reality. There are numbers of merits and demerits this social media has. Social media has emerged as the alternative media which gives voice to the neglected voiceless peoples.[5] social media through internet offers a new way for common people who had been deprived and have decided not to wait for revolution but to start living differently. The socio-culturally, economically and politically deprived people are willing to take control of their lives.[6] Such developments are taking place by virtue of social media which poses a challenge to internal vis-à-vis National Security. The aim of this paper is to study how social media has great relevance to National Security along with socio-cultural, economic and political aspects.

Negative Implication on Youth

Today's youth, are the citizens of tomorrow. The future of country, i.e. youth are always in conversation and communication with their friends and various groups. It is observed that they are constantly in touch not only with friends but also with unknown people through social networking sites. As a result of being constantly "online," they are becoming the subject of addiction, depression, stress and anxiety. Frequently, there are photographs, videos on media that contain violence and negative things which affect the behaviour of the youths. Youngsters waste lots of time on social sites which also affect their mental and physical well-being. Owing to this excessive use of social media, i.e. Internet, WhatsApp, Facebook, Instagram, YouTube, etc., by youngsters, they get distracted from their studies and other responsibilities. Such a disappointing picture may be harmful to the development process of a country. It poses a major hurdle for a healthy society vis-à-vis Healthy Nation.

Though there are advantages of social media, at the same time if we give a serious thought on the "future of the country" we will have to conclude that in the future society will have to face severe negative implications like health, physiological and domestic problems. Sharing every information, like updates on location, photographs and daily activities, could be very unsafe and in cases it gives a potential stalker and cyber bullies the information they need to track you. This is also an extreme case for caution with younger users.

Cyber Bullying

Cyber bullying is one of the major issues. In cyber bullying aggression occurs via electronic method especially through social media. Cyber bullies have an ability to hide their original identity and terrorize their victim through false identity. By virtue of disadvantages of social media society has to face numbers of problems. Some people share their images or videos on social sites that can provoke others to misuse it. Such videos, photos on media that contain violence and negative things can affect the behaviour of kids as well as youngster.[7] It is observed that befriending a stranger online who could be using a fake identity is extremely dangerous because you could end up giving your information to someone who could use it against you. In a social network, many people project different images when the reality is totally different.[8] Anti-social activities like kidnappings, murder, robbery, etc. are easily managed by criminals by acquiring details through social media.

Education

Education is a crucial and vital part of every society. Education sector has also been affected by social media. Because of social media students are losing their ability to engage themselves in face-to-face communication. Some of the bloggers and writers post inappropriate information on social sites which leads man towards the failure of education system.[9] Such inappropriate information may lead the students to the state of confusion and ultimately it will affect on their future. Information can be acquired from internet. Knowledge is different than information. Students they are more information oriented rather than knowledge.

Business

Trade and commerce also have certain challenges and problems that arise from the social media. Customers, friends and even followers are free to post their comments or opinions about a particular group of industry or company. Negative comments may demoralize the concerned company. In this age of information and technology a company or group of industries may be the victim of the hackers.[10] So trade and commerce sector has to face the above problems in addition to the cut-throat competition.

Terrorism

"Social Media" is exclusively used by the terrorist groups. Terrorism has proliferated worldwide in a very short period of time and has become as an international problem. Terrorists are intensively using social media; therefore it is proliferated very rapidly. For example, in Kashmir, through social media, terrorism attended for the expansion of their network. Various terrorist groups are using social media sites to spread their propaganda, raise funds, as well as to recruit and to train the new members. The fundamentalists are also using this social media as a platform to proliferate the prejudiced literature to create communal tension.[11] Social media is becoming an instrument for personal criminals and terrorist groups.

Cyber Terrorism

"Cyber Terrorism" is a new trend to destabilize the society and to create a confusion in hostile State. In cyber terrorism, the false information, i.e. rumours are being spread through internet deliberately to puzzle an enemy. In this context an example of cyber terrorism would be discussed as follows:

In April 2013, Syrian Electronic Army attacked the Associated Press Twitter account and sent the message as a "Breaking News", i.e. two explosions took place in the White House and President of U.S.A. Mr. Barack Obama got injured. Of course, this news was false. What were the immediate implications? Immediately the stock market plunged within a few minutes. As a result, the New York Stock Exchange dropped 1136 billion dollars.[12] So this episode of cyber terrorism destabilized the National Economy and Security along with turmoil at the global level. This example shows that how cyber terrorism can destabilize the nation's economy.

Conclusion

No doubt that there are a lot of advantages of social media, subject to its proper use. It is just like either science is a boon or bane? If it is used for a positive purpose then it would be a boon, but if it is used for a negative purpose then it could be bane. In view of the negative implications of social media, people have to restrict themselves to exclusive or necessary use of it. As far as security is concerned there are numbers of challenges/ problems arisen by the negative use of social media. Owing to vigourous use of social media, "Terrorism" is proliferated globally. The problems of "internet security" are also increasing due to social media. By virtue of the disadvantages of social media, criminalization tendency is developing in society.

Social Media has not only raised a question mark before National Security but it has also posed a serious threat to social security vis-à-vis internal security of a country. By disadvantages of social media our young generation is facing number of problems like stalking, hacking, plundering, psychological disturbances, suicide etc. In a nutshell social media has jeopardized the social vis-à-vis internal security i.e. core part of National Security. It is a phenomenon which presents both challenges and opportunities to society.

REFERENCES

1. General K.V. Krishnarao (1991), "Prepare or Parish", New Delhi: Lancer Publisher, pp. 6-7.
2. Raout, G. and Udgaonkar (2008), "History World Since World War-I (1918-1952)", New Delhi: Dimond Publication, P. 5.
3. Jacob Amedie, (2015), "The Impact of Social Media on Society", Santa Clara University, p. 1. Accessed at https://scholarcommons.scu.edu/engl_176/2/ on 1 February 2019.
4. Social media Overview, Communications and Marketing, Tufts University, accessed at https://communications.tufts.edu/marketing-and-branding/social-media-overview/#:~:text=Social%20media%20refers%20to%20the,Snapchat%2C%20YouTube%20and%20Vimeo%20accounts on 3 February 2019.
5. Kaur, Rakshinder (2018), "Role of Education in Developments of Human Values", Vol. 56 (27): 25-26.
6. Ray, Narain, Ash (2015), "Impact of social media on Society", New Delhi: Institute of Social Sciences, p. 3.
7. Siddiqui, Shabnoor and Singh, Tajinder (2016), "social media Its Impact with Positive and Negative Aspects," *International Journal of Computer Applications Technology and Research*, Vol. 5 (2), p. 74.
8. Amedie op. cit., p. 10.
9. Siddiqui and Singh op. cit. p. 72.
10. Ibid., p. 73.
11. Divya Marathi Special Nashik (M.S.) 19 September 2018.
12. Amedie op. cit., p. 14.

11

Impact of Social Media on Conflict Prevention and Peace

Dr. Saeideh Shariati Najafabadi

Introduction

This chapter presents evidence on how media development policies and programs can help prevent insecurity and violent conflict, and contribute towards peace. While there is increasing recognition given to the importance of media and its positive and negative potential in relation to conflict, there is relatively little accessible evidence. In recent years, the importance of a free, professional and plural media in contributing to good governance has gained traction in the international development community. A vibrant media gives people free flowing access to information, enables dialogue, encourages people to express their views, prompts greater political participation and encourages accountability.

Media, Local and Global Influence

Each conflict must be understood in the context of its own political, social and cultural context in addition to its specific media system. Conflicts today are, in many cases, more complex and multidimensional than ever before. The conflict cycle is a circular, dynamic process with several phases including various levels of diplomatic efforts to maintain peace in the run-up to war. The peace process that follows a ceasefire is also its own cycle including peace negotiations, signing of treaties and agreements, monitoring, prevention of lapsing into renewed conflict, and reconciliation. Elections also mark crucial phases in the cycle. Some researchers believe that there is not yet sufficient empirical evidence to confirm or reject claims that media promotes or prevents conflict and there is a reliance on anecdotal evidence to illustrate the media's positive impact on democracy and governance. While media and communication sectors sometimes create the conditions for sustainable political settlements, at other times they undermine the chances of them.

Social Media puts the audience as both content creators and consumers. Mass media (newspapers, TV, radio) is often perceived as less inclusive by virtue of being controlled by gatekeepers such as editors who decide whose voices and opinions will be heard. But social media (online blogs, Facebook, Twitter, etc.), can create "filter bubbles" exposing people only to content that supports their pre-existing beliefs, thereby polarizing public opinion.

The diffusion of internet, mobile and social media have moved us to "horizontal networks of interactive communication that connect local and global in chosen time" (Castells 2007).

Today local information can move rapidly across borders to reach audiences around the globe. This has the potential to fan conflict because different nations have different notions of what may and may not be said. At the same time, global media networks have significant influence on local audiences, resulting in a blend of global, local and 'glocal' information systems.

The velocity of today's communications often means a journalist's ability to assess critically what is happening is reduced as is the possibility of maintaining a balanced distance from events, leading to a horrible (and potentially dangerous) cycle of misinformation. Expressing observations and opinions in soundbites and tweets and avoiding rational discourse and analysis can fan conflict. The accelerating speed of communications can have positive as well as negative consequences for conflict management.

Roles of Media in Conflict Prevention and Promotion

The introduction of the virtual dimension and easily accessed and operated technologies changed the power balance between states, media and civilians. Today, civilians have more power to influence political processes; however the control over social media platforms remains commercial and sometimes political.

Media giants increased their power significantly as they control the "new oil" – Data.

Peace-builders who aspire to work efficiently in this new reality must understand what are the social media's sources of power are and how they can use them in their work.

The social media has an important contribution to make to the strengthening of peace and international understanding and in countering racialism, apartheid and incitement to war. Some are as follows:

- **It brings together different groups to discuss issues:** The media can be an effective tool to build relationships. It can support greater understanding and cohesion between people who consider themselves different from one another. It can give voice to the most marginalized in society. It can serve as a mediator between political parties especially in situations where there is no other means of communication particularly during conflict and post-conflict reconciliation.
- **Helps improve governance:** Fact-based, independent, transparent, accountable and impartial reporting can serve to hold officials accountable and make public administrations more transparent. It enables citizens to be active stakeholders, to understand policies and use the impartial information provided to exercise their human rights. All of these are critical for conflict prevention.
- **Increases knowledge of complex issues:** These include issues such as corruption, political injustice, marginalization, lack of economic opportunity and struggles with identity that may drive violent extremism. It can help people critically think about and discuss these issues.

- **Provides early warning:** Media can provide early warning of potential conflicts and possibly create pressure to address the conflict
- **Outlet to express emotions:** Media can allow people to express their fears and frustrations and share experiences and advice with others. It can also link people with power holders, enabling open communication and dialogue.
- Motivator for peace: The media can motivate people to take action and to participate in community events. But the media's impact on behaviour change is complex. It is more likely to work on attitudes and opinions that shape behaviours rather than directly affecting people's actions.

Additional best practices that should be ensured in any media and conflict prevention activity, project or programme include:

Ensure safety of media workers: None of this work can be pursued if media workers are unable to work in safety without being threatened, harassed or killed. Practitioners should be proactive with regard to safety and should address this early in the conflict process and not at the height of a conflict.

Do no harm: As discussed, the media have the potential to foment violence and spread hatred so all interventions should be implemented with this in mind and with attention to the context, the media sub-system and the interplay between the two. Interventions must be very carefully monitored and adjusted as necessary.

Build linkages with other institutions: Much of the work with media in conflict management to date has focused on the media sector itself rather than examining its interplay with other sub-systems and the greater system overall. It is crucial to build key linkages between peace-building and state-building institutions and media institutions, thereby supporting more effective media development in post-conflict environments. For example, media-military dialogues can be useful for building trust and understanding between those two sectors and beyond to the communities they serve.

Pursue integrated research and monitoring, evaluation and learning: There is a significant lack of evidence that shows causal impact of media interventions. Despite their importance, conducting rigorous impact evaluations continues to be a challenge for many development and peace-building programs. In some cases this is due to resources, in others a lack of foresight while others accept the difficulties of conducting such evaluations in fragile contexts.

In countering aggressive war, racialism, apartheid and other violations of human rights which are inter alia spawned by prejudice and ignorance, the social media, by disseminating information on the aims, aspirations, cultures and needs of all peoples, contributes to eliminate ignorance and misunderstanding between peoples, to make citizens of a country sensitive to the needs and desires of others, to ensure the respect of the rights and dignity of all nations, all peoples and all individuals without distinction of race, sex, language, religion or nationality and to draw attention to the great evils which afflict humanity, such as poverty, malnutrition and diseases, thereby promoting the formulation by States of the policies best able to promote the reduction of international tension and the peaceful and equitable settlement of international disputes.

Conclusion

With so much choice of news sources this should be a golden age for media. But in the shifting landscape where so many opposing voices are clamouring for attention, many people do not know who to trust.

In many fragile countries fact-based, independent, transparent, accountable and impartial reporting does not exist because of the business and political interests of media owners and the lack of pay and training for journalists. In others it is often subject to increased censorship, regulation and attack from parties that want to undermine its influence.

Media can be an instrument of conflict, used to incubate hatred and fan violence. It can reinforce the politics of division and identity rather than fostering social cohesion. It can bolster currently held belief systems rather than enlighten, inform and emancipate. Anyone, anywhere has the potential to play a role on a global scale with a local tweet or Facebook post or a blog. With that comes the obvious danger that an irresponsible, ill-informed, inflammatory comment can ignite violence.

Impartial media that gives voice to people from all sections of societies, including the most marginalized, can be an instrument of peace. It can arm them with knowledge that helps them make sense of events and take informed decisions rather than reacting to rumours.

It can uphold good governance by holding leaders to account, even eroding the power base of corrupt politicians. It can motivate people to take part in community events, peaceful demonstration and to vote responsibly. It can allow them to express and share pent up emotions and fears. It can connect them with others who perhaps hold different, opposing viewpoints to foster mutual understanding and greater social cohesion. It can also give them an opportunity to question power holders. It can provide early warnings of violence so people can avoid it. It can serve as a bridge between parties in peace negotiations.

The media is best placed to address the narratives and grievances of people involved in conflict and ensure that the voices heard are not only those of the elite or those that yell the loudest, but represent diversity.

REFERENCES

- Himelfarb, Sheldon. (2012). Social Media and Conflict Prevention, United States Institute of Peace. Accessed at https://www.usip.org/publications/2012/12/social-media-and-conflict-prevention on 15 December 2018.
- Beeston, Kym. (2014). How Social Media is changing the way we see conflict. Accessed at https://www.opendemocracy.net/opensecurity/kym-beeston/'sharing'-witness-is-social-media-changing-way-we-see-conflict on 12 January 2019.
- Makwana, Rajesh. (2016). A New Era of Global Protest Begins, Transcend Media Service. Accessed at https://www.transcend.org/tms/2016/01/a-new-era-of-global-protest-begins/ on 8 December 2018.
- Zeitzoff, Thomas. (2017). Tweets of Contention: How Social Media is Changing Political Conflict, Political Violence at a Glance. Accessed at http://politicalviolenceataglance.org/2017/08/30/tweets-of-contention-how-social-media-is-changing-political-conflict/ on 20 January 2019.
- Zeitzoff, Thomas. (2017). How Social Media is Changing Conflict. *Journal of Conflict Resolution*, vol. 61(9). Accessed at https://journals.sagepub.com/doi/10.1177/0022002717721392 on 18 January 2019.
- Castells, Manuel. (2007), Communication, Power and Counterpower in the Network Society, Vol. 1, *International Journal of Communication*, pp. 238-266.

12

Fake News: A Threat to Social Harmony and Peace

Dr. Gunratna Sontakke

Introduction

Fake news has existed for a very long time, nearly the same amount of time as news began to circulate widely after the printing press was invented in 1439. (Jacob, 2016). Fake news is not new, however it came to the fore in 2016 and later became a matter of concern for several governments across the globe, thanks to internet and social media. In India, fake news has become a tool to spread political propaganda and misinformation which can lead to violence and mistrust among people. When the term 'fake news' came into public notice, it was simply perceived as social media posts with rather incredible stories. However, it is more than what was imagined.

Fake news indeed is not just a post that has been liked, shared or followed; rather it is a powerful technique for spreading cyber propaganda with its dominant and far reaching effect. Lately, it is turning out to be one of the greatest threats to democracy, free debate and discussion.

Fake news is the promotion and propagation of news articles through social media. These articles are promoted in such a way that they appear to be spread by other users, as opposed to being paid-for advertising. The news stories distributed are designed to influence or manipulate users' opinions on a certain topic towards certain objectives (Lion Gu, Vladimir Kropotov and Fyodor Yarochkin).

How Does it Work?

WhatsApp is easy to handle, even people in rural parts of India can operate it very well. It can spread fake news at a startling speed to huge number of people.

Plummeting data prices and cheap 4-G enabled smartphones have put the social media in the hands of many people coming online for the first time.

Such new users are vulnerable to the kind of online manipulation that people more familiar with the internet would detect. According to a research WhatsApp usage can exacerbate groupthink, sometimes mobilising groups into acts of violence.

In an extensive report published recently, researchers from the BBC studying the spread of fake news in India found that WhatsApp groups encourage 'tightness' among users. "WhatsApp usage is about validation of one's beliefs and identities through sharing of news and information," the report says.

"This information ecosystem enables 'homophily'—birds of a feather flocking together. This characteristic of WhatsApp usage, which differs from Facebook because it is not driven algorithmically, could begin to explain why the platform has lead to mobilization in the cause of violence," researchers say.

Mob Violence at Rainpada

Five men were beaten to death by a raging mob in Rainpada village of Dhule district in Maharashtra. (July 1, 2018)

The five victims had arrived in the village earlier that day at around 9 am on a bus from Solapur to attend a Sunday Market. The men sat under a tree not far from where they had gotten off from the bus and, as they ate, handed a biscuit to a young girl. Their interaction with the girl quickly attracted the attention. Soon the crowd began to gather with people demanding answers from the men. And then a large mob had beaten them to death.

About a week before the victims arrived the village, rumors/fake news circulated on WhatsApp warning bands of kidnappers roving the area and infiltrating villages to snatch young children. In one grim version of the rumor, the children's organs were harvested and sold.

The police believe a video helped stoke fear and unease. It shows photos of pale, lifeless children laid out in rows, half covered in sheets. A voiceover warned parents to be vigilant and on the lookout for child snatchers.

It was found that the photos used in that video were of children killed in Syria during a chemical attack in 2013. The five victims in Rainpada were part of a string of killings linked to messages spread on WhatsApp.

Police and government officers estimate that more than 24 people have been killed by mobs, though no official tally is being kept. India Spend, a data journalism outlet, pegs the figure at 33 killed in 69 incidents of mob violence between January 2017 and July 2018.

In response WhatsApp reduced the number of contacts or groups a user could forward a message to five.

Post-Pulwama

Fake pictures of body parts of martyrs were circulated by some miscreants to invoke hatred among people. "It has been noticed that on social media some miscreants are trying to circulate fake picture of body parts of our martyrs to invoke hatred while we stand united. Please DO NOT circulate/share/like such photographs or posts," stated CRPF India on its twitter handle.

Post Air-strike

Videos of previous air-shows and photos of crashing fighter jets were being peddled from both the countries as latest.

Communal Fake News

Let's now see some of the communal fake news that made rounds on the social media in different parts of the country. Such fake news have potential to generate negative thoughts about some groups or communities and can lead to violence, hence disturbing the peace and social harmony.

- Fake news of nine-year old rescued from being sexually assaulted by 'Sajid'
  "A 9yr old girl was saved 4pm rape by alert people. Guy, who was caught with kid, is Sajid. M/s @Uppolice please arrest this guy Sajid and make him spend some hours in jail" This message was circulated along with a video in which a girl child is seen crying and a young man is thrashed by passers-by. The perpetrator's name is not Sajid but Gokul Ramdas.The persons who tweeted this message with video were followed by PM Modi and Union minister Piyush Goyal.
- Fake news of March by Muslims demanding release of Mandsaur rape accused
  Photoshopped image of madrassa teacher portraying Islam as superior to Hinduism. Actually in this madrassa Sanskrit was being taught and teacher was comparing some words in Sanskrit with Islam on a black board.
- False claim of a woman's hair chopped off for not wearing burqa
  Communally provocative misinformation was spread in Karnataka prior to assembly polls in 2018.
- Pakistan flag waved at Congress rally in Karnataka
  WhatsApp, Facebook, Twitter rather the social media was abuzz with the claim that Pakistani flag was waved at a rally by the Congress party in North Belgaum. This message along with a video of the rally in which green coloured flag can be seen, was spread on the social media. The flag that was waved at this rally was not the Pakistani flag. This is a fact that the flag of IUML (Indian Union Muslim League), which is different from the flag of Pakistan.

Online Political Propaganda

In India a large number of people use WhatsApp and it is a common way to connect with friends, family, and the community through private and public groups. The popularity of the Facebook-owned messaging application is why distorted campaigns breed on it.There are instances wherein political campaigners in India hired public relations or consulting firms to spread online propaganda.

From completely false and partially-true misleading narratives to hate and bigotry, everything is circulated in the closed encrypted world of India's most popular instant messenger, with over 230 million active users. According to Lokniti-CSDS Mood of the Nation (MOTN) survey (2017), around one-sixth of WhatsApp users in India said they were members of a group started by a political leader or party.

In the run-up to the upcoming 2019 election, the ruling BJP has reportedly set up thousands of WhatsApp groups to directly reach out to their electorate. BJP's president Amit Shah is apparently a member of each one of them in an attempt to stop the spread of fake news. However, during the 2014 elections, when social media first emerged as a pivotal campaign tool for Indian political parties. Even during polls in some states this year, WhatsApp reportedly housed rampant misinformation from several political actors. The chatting app isn't the only source of fake news in India.

Twitter

On Twitter, some researchers discovered evidence of political parties using bots to boost their follower counts, or to retweet, like, or share content that supported their campaigns. "The automated accounts allow you to reach more people, and if you can generate trends, you can generate truth," a research said.

The recent purge of fake accounts on Twitter, where Prime Minister Modi lost 300,000 followers and Congress chief Rahul Gandhi lost 17,000, speaks of how widespread bot activity is among India's political leaders.

A Recent Study

In a recent study by Samarth Bansal, Kiran Garimella and Dean Eckles (2018) monitored public WhatsApp groups that are open to the public to check the extent of fake news. They joined these through links publicized on the internet. At the outset the study points out "WhatsApp is a black box for content. It is nearly not possible to track misinformation in the WhatsApp sphere as the content is end-to-end encrypted and no one can and should not access private chats at scale. Given this restriction, we decided to monitor 'public' WhatsApp groups that are open to the public."

They manually classified each WhatsApp group in our dataset with its party affiliation: of the total, they identified 693 pro-BJP groups; 156 pro-Congress; and the rest voice support for various regional parties and religious groups. To be sure, it is not known how many of these groups are managed by the office-bearers of political parties, though there is some evidence of centralisation.

For instance, around 400 groups in their database were created by just 10 phone numbers. Overall, 1, 49,305 people were members of the groups we monitored. 79,781 members (53 per cent of all members) sent at least one message; 31,459 (21 per cent) shared at least one image.

Anti-Congress Fake News

Communal polarisation was the major theme of anti-Congress misinformation in the dataset: it aims to establish that the Congress party only cares about Muslims.

Then there is bigotry, with messages that ask people to connect the dots and rethink whether Rahul Gandhi is actually a Hindu by questioning the religiosity of his ancestors.

The narrative begins with Jawaharlal Nehru, India's first prime minister and Gandhi's great-grandfather. "By education, I'm an Englishman, by views an internationalist, by culture a Muslim and a Hindu only by accident of birth," reads a quote attributed to Nehru in a newspaper clipping. Nehru never said this.

The next target in line is Feroz Gandhi, husband of former Prime Minister Indira Gandhi and Rahul Gandhi's grandfather. The messages repeat the long-standing false rumour that Feroze Gandhi was a Muslim, in contrast with the well-documented fact that he belonged to a Parsi family.

Then, questions are raised about the marriage of Rajiv and Sonia Gandhi, his parents: "Mother and father got their marriage registered in

Delhi church as a Christian couple. Son claims himself as a janeudhari Hindu. Can there be a bigger joke?" reads one message. A fact-checked by SM Hoax Slayer showed that this claim is wrong.

Another says: "How can a son of a Parsi man and Christian woman be a Hindu? Have you ever thought about this?"

Suchrumours have been a part of the political discourse for long period of time and are constantly fed to Indians. Put this into the political context and see what it indicates: the strategy to portray Congress as an anti-Hindu party, a theme BJP has leveraged to mobilise the Hindu electorate and consolidate the vote in their favour. In fact, several images shared in the groups the researchers monitored make an explicit call for Hindus to unite to defeat the Congress.

Anti-BJP Fake News

Anti-BJP fake news try to show PM Narendra Modi and his party as corrupt. Clippings tagged with 'News Express' it is not clear who runs this organisation, and if there is any real organisation with that name ran a headline saying: "Rafale scam: Former President of France Francois Hollande says PM Modi is a thief." Hollande never said this."RBI accepts that demonetisation was a wrong decision. It is a nine lakh crore rupees scam," reads an image post, attributing the statement to Urjit Patel, former governor of the Reserve Bank of India.

"Narendra Modi government is the most corrupt government in Asia, says Forbes magazine".

"India becomes bankrupt, according to a shocking revelation by the World Bank. India owes 1, 31,000 million dollars". None of this is true.

Corrective Measures by WhatsApp

WhatsApp has taken some measures last year. It took out full-page advertisements in Indian newspapers to fight misinformation, and started labelling forwarded content and limited the number of forwards to five messages only. In February, the company said it has communicated to Indian political parties that WhatsApp 'is not a broadcast platform', 'not a place to send messages at scale" and accounts that 'engage itself in automated bot behaviour' will be banned. WhatsApp has deleted two million accounts per month for the past three months on that account.

Conclusion

Misinformation, fake news could be spread through social media to huge number of people at startling speed which may led to communal disharmony and violence. Rumors/fake news has led to a string of killings linked to messages spread on WhatsApp in several parts of country.

Fake news has grown manifold, a large portion of it is dominated by information which is communal in nature and and provoking in tone, seeking to divide the society on religious lines. Some correctives measures have been taken by the government and the service providers on the internet to fight the misinformation.

People should be educated how to spot fake news and not to believe it and spread it. They should be educated to validate or verify the news with authentic sources. Government should bring laws and regulations.

REFERENCES

1. Roozenbeek J, & Linde S (2019), *The Fake News Game: Actively Inoculating Against the Risk of Misinformation*, Accessed at https://www.cam.ac.uk/sites/www.cam.ac.uk/files/fakenews_latest_jrr_aaas.pdf on 25 February 2019.
2. Goswami M (2018), *Fake News and Cyber Propaganda: A study of manipulation and abuses on social media* Accessed at https://www.researchgate.net/publication/326655516_Fake_News_and_Cyber_Propaganda_A_Study_of_Manipulation_and_Abuses_on_Social_Media on 2 March 2019.
3. Carson, J (2019), Fake news: What exactly is it – and how can you spot it?. Accessed at https://www.telegraph.co.uk/technology/0/fake-news-exactly-has-really-had-influence/ on 2 March 2019.
4. Bigelow, S (2018), Fake news, propaganda spread quickly on Social Media, 2018.Accessed at https://universe.byu.edu/2018/12/26/fake-news-influence-spreads-quickly-on-social-media/ on 2 March 2019.
5. McLaughlin, T. (2018), *How WhatsApp Fuels Fake News and Violence in Indi.* Accessed at, https://www.wired.com/story/how-whatsapp-fuels-fake-news-and-violence-in-india/ on 2 March 2019.
6. Bansal, S. and Garimella, K. (2019), *Fighting fake news: Decoding 'fact-free' world of WhatsApp.* Accessed at https://www.hindustantimes.com/india-news/decoding-fact-free-world-of-whatsapp/story-LQ79X96OOKrGo7MHuW3TMP.html on 2 March 2019.
7. Gu, Lion, Kropotov, Vladimir and Yarochkin, Fyodor (2017), The Fake News Machine: How Propagandists Abuse the Internet and Manipulate the Public. Accessed at https://www.trendmicro.com/vinfo/nl/security/news/cybercrime-and-digital-threats/fake-news-cyber-propaganda-the-abuse-of-social-media on 2 March 2019.

13

The New Forms of Media, Social Media and the Transformation of the Media Sphere-Chaos: Peace and Security

Col. Arunender Thakur

Introduction

The social platforms in civilised societies started way back in our civilisation. There is mention of social gatherings like various Sabhas,[1] Durbars, Shastrarthas[2] and confidential message system since Vedic[3] times. Sri Hanuman[4] taking the message of Sri Rama[5] to his wife in Lanka, Sri Angad[6] taking the message of Sri Ram to Ravan[7] before war, Sri Krishna[8] taking the message of Pandavas[9] to Kauravas[10] before war, etc., are instances mentioned in our sacred scriptures. In other parts of the world, there are religions based on messages passed on by the God/ Almighty/Allah/Bhagwan to their chosen disciples who further passed it on to their followers. The Confidentiality, Integrity and Security of the messages were important. In Vedic times, the Shastrarthas/discourses in Public domain were taken very seriously and most of the time, the loser had to become a disciple of the winner along with all his/her disciples, and he/she had to leave his/her ideology and imbibe the winner's ideology. The times changed, the country was invaded several times, openness gave way to restricted gathering, and when Britishers came in, contrary to the perceptions[11] now a days, they almost stopped any open/logical discussion in the country, systematically dismantling the robust established system. Times changed again, giving way to Industrial revolution, World Wars, Freedom, Machines, Computers, Smartphones and the Internet. The world has been shrinking since.

What Makes the Threat/Rise of Social Media Real

The social media companies like Google (including YouTube, Gmail, etc.), Facebook (including Whattsapp, Instagram, etc.), Yahoo (including Yahoo mail), Twitter, etc., have become giant companies employing lakhs of people worldwide and have a multi-billion dollar turnover. All such companies under the garb of providing free seamless social interaction platforms are in many ways indulging into changing lives of people as they desire. These companies have access to user data—who they are, their complete profile, their posts, their leanings, contact details, photo galleries, their movement records even when offline, their choices, passwords for different services including banking sites, their list of searches, etc, the list is never ending and so is their storage capacity. Anything that one sees/puts on any social media platform remains there for eternity. Even after the post is deleted, it remains in the server/storage medium of the service provider for some time as per stated policy[12] of the service provider. In the garb of research and providing efficient service, the companies have also stated in their privacy policy that if required they can post a comment/picture/advertisement/video to anybody from the user's side. The social media sphere[13] has got much bigger than what we can imagine, at present almost 500 million people of India have internet connection and approximately 400 million have smart phones. A person can get a data pack of 1 GB per day at cheap rate. This high speed internet service has facilitated sharing of large information between people. It has the power to influence people and the effects of it can be seen in the society. Not only has it brought people closer, but it also has been the cause of many tragedies.

These social media giants have a major database on every user with a smartphone and internet connection. This large database fed through different algorithms and artificial intelligence systems churns out lots of possibilities and outcomes for providing data feeds for researches, experimentation, probing, etc., without anyone knowing about it. Companies can track your browsing habits to display personalised ads that keep popping up, send business mails (some could be fraud) to, share news and videos with you. The alleged selling of data,[14] manipulation of content shown (including business and electoral) are part of this elaborate game plan. All are being carried out by these social media giants just for Profit and Power (controlling lives of people without them knowing).

Expanding Social Media: Disruptive Technology

In the nineties, the media meant Newspaper, TV, magazines and social gatherings at villages/towns. The positive outcomes of this system was that people had independent minds to make choices, had access to limited content (beneficial to the society as a whole), had more time for being social, developed reading habits, debated and discussed face to face, etc. There was less propagation of negativity in the society. The negatives of this system was restricted contents on media (media was heavily controlled), less awareness, low transparency in government dealings and decision-making processes.

The common man did not have a voice and was not paid heed to. There was no channel of regular feedback to accurately determine the effectiveness of government schemes. Yet something was brewing in the nineties (developments in computers, cell phones, internet, social media platforms, onslaught of cable television networks), the cascading effects of these new inventions was beyond anyone's imagination. The disruption was just on the horizon, it just wasn't visible to anyone yet. So when these inventions came in to our world, they just got absorbed in the unsuspecting society and in the lives of people, slowly but steadily. Earlier the technologies were costlier, but as the time passed, these became much cheaper, and today they are cheaper than some daily necessities. Internet got into the lives of the people; new businesses emerged based on this platform. The gadgets like computers, laptops, smartphones, etc., kept evolving with latest technology, and, giving them extremely tough competition was social media/associated software, which was progressing leaps and bounds at the same time resulting in development of Blogs, Facebook, Google, Yahoo,YouTube, etc.

By 2010, within just ten years of these technologies coming into people's lives, one could see lots of people getting connected to each other (people connecting to their long lost friends, various groups and social groups were created), mushrooming of lots of TV channels, explosion in content development to cater for these different social media platforms. There were major Civil Society revolutions which toppled Governments, for e.g. Egypt, Libya, and to some extent India, etc. From 2010, till date the technology (both hardware and the social media platforms) have evolved so much that now the Smartphone is a household item(necessary item), Whats Report on Usage of Internet and Smartphones App, Facebook, E-mails, Twitter, etc., have become household names, and, have become giant business houses with turnovers in billions of dollars.

The discussion is always about positives and negatives of social media but never on the chaos or the disruptive effects it is having on lives of the people and what lies ahead of this all. The privacy policy[15] of Facebook (FB) states that the data as on FB will be used for research and innovation for betterment of services, the information from their studies/ data and services will be utilised by them and can also collaborate with others (third parties also) on research, the user will have no claim on ownership of data which they put on FB (and grant FB the license to use and modify that input as they like). Moreover, if that content is not as per law of country the user can be booked by government and not FB, permission to use username, profile picture, information on relation, accounts, advertisements and sponsored contents, download and install updates on the device, change terms and conditions whenever they like, collection of information, photos, messages, views, groups, pages connected, usage patterns, etc., and use it for their own research and propagation purposes. Collect device information (OS, hardware, signals, GPS locations, camera, microphone access, malware, cookies datas, etc) for their usage, they also get data from their partners when users are not on FB, etc. Most of the other social media platforms (Google, Yahoo, WhatsApp, Twitter, etc) have more or less the same policy for controlling the people's accounts as stated in their respective privacy policies. Without agreeing to all these policies, nobody is registered at any social media platform.

The statements of these Privacy policies are simply stating that whoever joins their platforms; pledges to lay open all of his/her private life and will be sharing all information with that social media willingly. Information is power, and all related information about all registered person is held and monitored by these social media giants, and this has been going on for ages. The plea of these social media platforms for collecting and monitoring all the data is that they want to help the users have good and fast experience in connecting with and sharing their posts with others. These companies are mining all the data for their profit and all users let them do this willingly, just so that all can use their sites to stay connected.

Social media has slowly and stealthily become seamlessly integrated into our lives. Fifteen years back, nobody knew that there will be a handheld phone through which one can potentially communicate to so many people at the same time, share photos, ideas, videos, etc., live in real time. No one knew that one could compliment/ abuse any celebrity/ politician/anyone on his/her social media page. No one knew that the government could advertise its schemes to one and all through social media; no one knew that we would be addicted to social media. No one knew that companies would be paying people to do research on social media; no one knew that political parties would be spending more on social media campaigns than any other campaigns for winning elections.

The influence of social media sphere is affecting people's thoughts and behaviours in a major way, for e.g. Cambridge Analytica.[16] Case of allegedly influencing leanings of people on social media by sourcing such data from FB, reportedly authenticated cases of sharing people's data by FB, Google, etc., with other business houses, reported cases of hacking of personal data from such social media sites. Dark Web[17] social media sphere is also expanding in a major way, wherein unknown/ unidentified people indulge in all sorts of unlawful activities like hacking, buying of any data, hacking for ransom, hijacking, contract killing, stealing of financial information, etc. Making unsuspecting people part of their social/logical/ research bound/medical/validation projects to launch/implement their new offerings. The technologies (both hardware and software) are changing at such a fast pace that new smartphones/ software are getting out dated within 6 months, various platforms of social media are getting more and more user friendly thus more addictive. Various TV (news and video contents) channels have lost their TRPs to the social media platforms and are unable to sustain themselves and all the business houses and politicians have realised the importance of this medium in the lives of people.

Seemingly Positive – Negative Effects

Seemingly Positive Effects	*Negative/Chaotic Effects*
Brings long lost friends, acquaintances, relatives together; type a name and FB connects to that person. It is a great feeling of being back in time, and this connection now stays forever.	The unending game of connecting starts, the moment one joins any social media platform. After this first step, there is no control, other friends are suggested by their algorithms and one adds them, then another and another, so on. One gets one's groups of different kinds but even in a peer group who 20 years back were great friends, would have different priorities now, would be at different stages of life and facing different problems. However, 99.9 per cent of the people connected on social media would post positive things only that also for validation, which gives rise to comparisons which in turn lead to jealousy and envy in minds of other people which eventually gives rise to depression.[18] No one's life is as perfect as is often shown on Facebook.
Present generation is internet savvy generation (technology is flowing in all their veins), they are all on one social media platform or the other, are well connected, are into various kinds of entertainment avenues (like videos, memes, photos, movies on social media, etc.) and are in constant real time conversation with each other. They have such websites and inspiring people whom they can follow for motivation, they help to develop social skills of sorts, help in developing reading and writing skills.	Young people/children spend twice amount of time on social media than at school, indulge in multitasking, being on social media, listening to music and working on some project or studying at the same time, thus reducing their attention span, leading to distorted body images, risky and skewed behaviour and low scores. Everyone has made make mistakes, often because of lack of maturity in their younger days, however, on social media the things (posts) stay forever, thus, no second chance is given to anyone.
Affects lifestyle in positive ways and encourages young population to be more involved in decision making for the society/country/ politics.	The comparisons start here again, due to urge of posting all positive things and attraction to material things give rise to jealousy and envy and thus resulting into depression, sleep disorders and change in moods and bad life choices. All the activities of any person can be checked by the government agencies, the employers or anyone else having the wherewithal or motivation for checking. Young people including

	children place more importance on emotions like acceptance in their peer group, need to be seen (reading of posts by others) on social media, need to be liked (liking of posts), etc. These facets consume more time and effort and at most of the time lead to loneliness and depression. Makes young people emulate a way of life often that is not natural to them or comfortable for them or their families (socially and financially) without understanding the long-term implications of their decisions.
Physiological and psychological[19] changes to mind in a positive manner by offering solace in self, by feeling needed and feeling connected, etc.	Most of the choices which pop up on social media platforms, including Google, have the search results based on their choice rather than of the user's choice, so in a way dictating what one can see/learn about. Fulfils the need for intermittent variable rewards by checking the social media platforms several times a day. This act comes from the 'Fear of Missing Out' on something important that a person will miss if he/she does not see the updates every now and then. Fulfils the need for social approval (FB keeps popping up the DP change or information on photos, etc., to other people, obligation being the main factor) Fulfils emotion of reciprocity by approving the posts of those who approve theirs (tit for tat). It puts the mind into believing that it can satisfy itself by feeding information from bottomless pits. Infinite feeds and auto-play feature of these social media platforms (FB, YouTube, etc) can keep one engaged till eternity. Instant interruption feature at these sites prompts the users to at least have a look, thus utilising behavioural instinctive for profit generation by these sites.
Freedom of expression in that whatever one wants to put, though not offensive or obscene, but photos, videos, comments in whatever language at whatever time of the day for everybody to see in real time. Most of the people at any level can make a comment or statement in their personal capacity, but if the same is done by some celebrity/politician or the comment is different, lot of people see the post and show their likeness for the posts. People become followers of such people in no time. Thus has given a larger platform to all.	Organisations/certain people are on the lookout for people who have a different ideology, target those people in assistance with AI and Bots and (can) trap them for personal gains, thus empowering malicious behaviours. He/she objects (posts negative about the comment), and with the reach of social media is such that lot of people (if they also do not like a particular comment), within no time the social media will be flooded by negative comments. Certain unscrupulous elements involve Bots and AI[20] to do this negative propagation of negative replies, known as trolling. Many suicides have reportedly happened due to this.

Seemingly Positive Effects	*Negative/Chaotic Effects*
Dare games[21] are fads and adrenaline pumping dares are the status symbols promoted by certain section of social media. It gives a high to people doing the same and sharing the events on social media. For e.g. Blue whale, Ki-Ki challenge, etc.	More often than not all these dare games lead to accidents and loss of lives. Young adults lack the required discerning ability to make the correct decisions. More often than not, by the time help arrives it is too late for them.
World is flat[22]. Social media promotes talent by giving an opportunity to all. Opportunity is not limited to rich people in big cities only. Anyone with talent can make a video, upload, the content and if its good will be seen by many due to the reach of the social media. Lot of talents have been discovered by people/groups/business houses for their projects for movies, songs, events, etc. Thus, stars are born within no time on social media on pure talent basis. They also prove to be an effective media for promotion of the culture and related things like festivals, cuisine etc. These social media platforms are a boon for getting new jobs and opportunities.	There are undesirable elements too who are on the look-out for children/young/susceptible people wanting to make a name for themselves and lure them into wrong directions/professions/activities. Since all data about oneself is available on the net on various social media platforms, instead of the qualification for the job, other attributes like religious, political, sexual leanings, teamwork, integrity, etc., take more weightage for deciding the fate of the candidate.
People are getting connected, are talking via text, photos, videos, sharing issues and events and having real time arguments over things as per personal choices.	People are losing communication skills[23] (skill to talk/communicate face to face, make meaningful conversations), they are forgetting social etiquettes and manners, ability to work as a team. This indulging into social media sphere gives rise to Narcissism and losing of empathy and sympathy as well, for e.g. nowadays, people indulge in making video of a dying person on roadside instead of taking him/ her to a hospital.
This social media has helped business houses a lot in marketing[24] their products, since reach of these platforms is to a wide array of people. There is better understanding of customers, promotion of products is all over the world, information on competitors is available, networking opens more avenues, new insights are received from dealers/users and complete information on products is available. Companies can get real time feedback on their products from the consumers and also consumers can get reviews of the products from other verified customers.	These sites continuously monitor one's search patterns, based on which they keep showing advertisements regularly to buy things they one does not actually need. They create artificial needs by constantly bombarding users with images of stuff which according to them will make their life more meaningful. After one buys, the next process starts immediately as the human mind starts craving for next thing and social media is there to oblige. These unplanned buying get people eventually into debt traps. They are promoting mindless consumerism.

Videos and talks of renowned doctors and medical institutions, network of various groups of professors, new researches available online, bonding of doctors with patients, real-time monitoring and feedback are available for all to see and to follow necessary guidelines and imbibe healthy lifestyles.	Videos of normal doctors/ quacks/ unscrupulous elements posing as doctors are also on the web – leading to self-medication (incorrect self-diagnosis)/ unsupervised medication, complication and death in certain cases. Breach of privacy is also an issue. Gullible public thinks that everything that they see on these sites are well researched and by extension reliable.
In education field, socialising, sharing knowledge, updating self, learning from various sources, connecting with teachers, open knowledge sources in media gives an added edge to the students.	The considerable use of social media by people, reduces learning and research capability, reduces real human content [26] in any study/research, reduce command over language and creative writing, time wastage, resulting in low grades, loss of motivation and effects health in a major way.
Socialising via seamless connectivity, education, help online, information updates, advertisements, pursuing of noble causes, helps in building communities, writers and bloggers to connect, groups for support, for positive goals and changes in the society.	The negative outcomes[26] are fake news, mobs take law in their own hands due to some politically/ communally charged video clip, more instances of frauds, prying into lives of people, honey traps, blackmailing, money laundering, black marketing, spreading negative agenda of anti-government people/groups, rise in depression cases, rise including divorces, and breaking up of relationships.
The transparency drive of government in highlighting all its schemes, their procedure and progress thereto on different social media platforms along with active discussion and feedback by general public has shaped up these schemes and prompted government for introduction of new schemes as well for the benefit of the society and the country. Positive examples in India are, changing mind set of people,[27] cleanliness by Swachh Bharat campaign, making Khadi village industries a profit making venture, involving citizens in decision-making process of the government, spreading of government welfare schemes, etc.	Cyber harassing, hacking, addiction, fraud, scam, negative effects on reputation (fast spread of false news/photos/data).Theft of data and influencing the decision making by flooding the feedback by designated Bots, AI, etc., affects decision making process of the government in a big way. The downside of this outreach and speed of spreading information through social media much outweighs its positive aspects, so much so that governments shut the internet and all the social media platforms, the moment they feel that any disruption is happening and to restrict the spread of negative or harmful ideas amongst people.Monitoring of social media gives insight to government agencies to fight crimes, at the same time it gives ideas to unwanted people/groups/institutions/business houses to exploit the huge information/data mine.

Near and Far Future: Possible Scenarios of Social Media Chaos

Keeping the facts discussed in mind while we keep pace with technological progress of the internet, and being aware of certain activities of companies involved in the Dark Web, the following future can be predicted. Seamless integration between various social media platforms like Facebook, WhatsApp, Instagram, Google, YouTube, banks, government apps, etc. The positives will be that people can use anything easily to communicate, pay, avail government subsidies, etc. Negatives will be that all the users' data will become more vulnerable. Any new technology/social media Company that comes up with more promising features will either be taken over or finished in no time.

Artificial Intelligence, Internet of things, Virtual reality, Augmented reality and biotechnologies will be employed in a major way to alter and control the minds of people through overt as well as subtle means. Entire lives of the people will be seamlessly integrated with AI, robots, household appliances, cars, trains, aircraft, offices, banks. Governments will be toppled more by social media use/misuse than by armed conflict. News will be created rather than reported. Real time being the buzzword. For the safety of the people, personal data of the citizens will be stored in a digital form, paid for and available for a predetermined time period after which it will be removed.

Dark Web social media will be flexing its muscles and will be in more common use for unscrupulous activities than it is now. The advanced technology will make us digitally handicapped.[28] People will expect processed information of all kinds presented to them duly analysed and processed for their consumption and will make us completely dependent on digital world. The categorisation of social media platforms is also undergoing a dynamic change, like, most of these platforms are getting together and are developing asymbiotic relationship between each other and one can seamlessly share data amongst many of them. Certain websites and technological companies are not overtly into social media, but are covertly making people follow their stories based on the data collected from the user data pattern Thus, sites such as Google, Wikipedia, Yahoo, Bing, etc., which are overtly into search engine and knowledge sharing business are also into shaping up opinions of people. These have contents made by users, mined from user's usage data; it is for users, as required by the company's policy which is dictated by profits and for becoming the power centre in all spheres. All in all, harms to well-being will outweigh the positives in the next decade. Technologies that were created to help us have become tools of surveillance, behavioural manipulation, and addiction.

Conclusion

The ability to both monitor and manipulate individuals is increasing every day. Over the past decade, technologies to track our online behaviour were developed and the next decade will see increased surveillance of our off-line behaviour. The combination of these technologies makes it possible for observers (Amazon, government, Facebook, etc.) to know what we are doing, what we like and how we react. The pace at which researches and associated advancements are happening regarding technologies and social media platforms, and the way these technological giants are influencing the minds of general public, it is a daunting task to stop them. Ultimately, peace and security will be left far behind. Profit and power with certain big business houses will be the only thing remaining.

The invention of Bots (computer programs to copy human responses as one wants on social media and internet), Augmented reality (mixing reality with virtual dimension things/characters), Wearable devices to enhance capabilities as well as for Virtual Reality (VR), Alexa (virtual assistance of Amazon), Siri (virtual assistance of I-Phone) are already causing worries as they threaten our psychological, economic and political well-being. Certain big business houses (Microsoft, Apple, Jio, etc) and entrepreneurs are also on the job to create something much bigger than FB, Google, etc. How the platforms and technologies will shape up in future, what business models will drive the sales, social hives/minds created by AIs, Bots, Information aggregators, Algorithms amalgam of humans and Avatar (movie avatar fame) and programs which will be super smart, alive and autonomous are some of the glimpses of future that we are expecting and looking at.

Now is the only time we have, which is very less, since technology and associated activities including social media sphere is progressing by leaps and bounds trying to encircle the very purpose of our existence. If these advancements are left unchecked with loose and ineffective laws, without any ethics or moral checks chaos is what we should expect and chaos is what we will get.

REFERENCES

1. Rigvedaand Atharveda; Basham, "The Wonder that was India".
2. Ibid.
3. Ibid.
4. MN Dutt, " Prose Translation of the Complete Ramayana"; Maharishi Valmiki, " Ramayana"
5. Ibid.
6. Ibid.
7. Ibid.
8. Maharishi Ved Vyasa, " Mahabharata".
9. Ibid.
10. Ibid.
11. Tharoor, Shashi. 2017. "Inglorious Empire: What the British did to India", London: Hurst & Company.
12. Privacy and Data Policy of Facebook, Whattsapp, Google, Twitter, Youtube, etc as given on their websites.
13. Report on Usage of Internet and Smartphones, *The Economic Times*, 20 February 2018.
14. News Article, BBC, "Alleged Selling of Data by Social Media Platforms",19 December 2018.
15. Privacy and Data Policy of Facebook, Whattsapp, Google, Twitter, YouTube, etc., as given on their Websites.
16. *The Guardian* and *The New York Times* Coverage of the Case of Cambridge Analytica, 17 Mar 2018.
17. Paganini, Pierluigi and Amores, Richard. 2012. "The Deep Dark Web: The Hidden World: Volume 1, United States: CreateSpace Independent Publishing Platform
18. Farek A. El-Badawy and Yasmin Hashem, 2015, "The Impact of Social Media on the Academic Development of School Students", *International Journal of Business Administration*, Vol. 6 (1): 46-52.
19. Harris, Tristan. 2016. "How Technology is Hijacking Your Mind-from A Magician and Google Design Ethicist". Accessed at https://Timewellspot.Io on 3 February 2019.
20. Janarthanam, Srini. 2017. "Hands on Chatbots and Conversational UI Development," United Kingdom: Packt Publishing.
21. Danger Ahead: Social Media Dare Games. 2016. Accessed at Https:// Netsanity.Net/Danger-Ahead-social media- Dare Games/ on 10 January 2019.
22. Friedman, L, Thomas L. 2005. The World Is Flat: A Brief History of the Twenty-first Century, New York: Farrar, Straus and Giroux.
23. Akram, Waseem and Kumar, R. 2018. "A Study on Positive and Negative Effects of Social Media on Society", *International Journal of Computer Science and Engineering*, Vol. 5 (10): 347-354.
24. Farkud, Adi. 2016. "social media, Its Positive and Negative Implications on Society", Accessed at https:// Www// Researchgate.Net/ Publication/3100c8721 on 3 February 2019.
25. Department for Work & Pensions (DWP). 2014. "The Use of Social Media for Research and Analysis: A Feasibility Study, Oxford International Institute. Accessed

at file:///C:/Users/Comp-2/Downloads/Use-of-social-media-for-research-and-analysis-a-feasibility-study%20(1).pdf on 2 January 2019.

26. Henderson, Lance. 2015. "TOR and the Dark Art of Anonymity: How to Be Invisible from NSA Spying" United States: Createspace Independent Pub.
27. Shukla, Himanshu. 2015. "Management Guru Narendra Modi", New Delhi: Diamond Books.
28. Word Meaning, "Handicapped Without Digital Technologies". Accessed at Https://Www.Urbandictionary.Com on 27 February 2019.

14

Social Media and Peer Pressure: Impact on Peace and Security

Milad Ghiasi

Introduction to Peer Pressure

Peer pressure is the influence on individuals of their peers that motivates them to follow their peers by changing their values, behaviours or attitudes or do things that they otherwise wouldn't do. Peer pressure can result in either negative or positive effects and such kind of pressure can be generated anywhere like working atmospheres, classrooms, community of friends, family or even on the internet or social media. Therefore, effects of peer pressure in social media on people's behaviour, peace and security will be analysed in this chapter.

As it can be inferred from the chart, the circle of friends for all people is more or less same, which starts from families and close friends and so on. Through social media, these circles can be utilized positively to generate a great influence on people's behaviour and attitudes.

History and Preview of Internet Challenges with the Aim of Health

The concept of challenges using hashtags on Instagram, Facebook, etc., is another rage. The Ice bucket challenge on Instagram and Facebook

Figure 1: A Social Circle of a Person

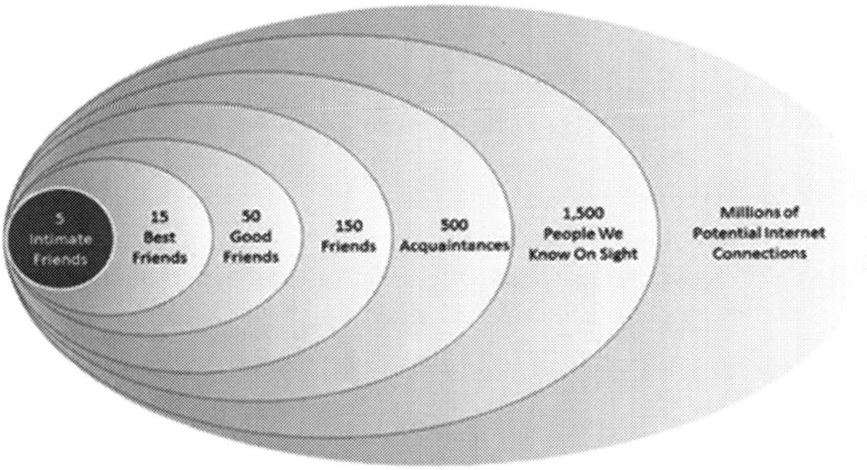

Source: Author's own compilation

took place in 2013 and in almost 1 year people all around the world joined it with the aim of creating awareness about ALS, also known as motor neuron disease and in the US as Lou Gehrig's disease.

In that challenge which is a video challenge, participants nominate their friends to either perform the challenge or donate 100 dollars to ALS research and patients.The purpose was to spread awareness about ALS which was a successful challenge that collected almost 4 million dollars by the end of 2014, and ALS research centre reported more than 70000 donors only in 2014.Many famous faces and celebrities also took part in the challenge to spread the awareness which helped in its promotion and getting more people to joined it.

How to Promote the Challenge

Many famous faces from international movie stars, to many politicians and famous businessmen participated in the Ice Bucket Challenge among which, the United States President Barack Hussein Obama, Bill Gates, Mark Zuckerberg are the most known ones.On the other hand, a great number of Hollywood and Bollywood stars had a role in the mentioned challenge.

Participating in the challenge was again about peer pressure for many people around the world. Challenges are often a great way to get yourself in front of influencers and potential customers, or to promote a social cause or idea, grow your reach, build your brand, etc. For example, a challenge for peace would be a good idea. In it people all over the world can show a white flog to the camera as a symbol of peace and brotherhood. Everyone can start a new movement or a new challenge and pass it on the neighbours and so on till it becomes a rage worldwide. To make it more creative something can be added to the action by each user as he/she wants, like a piece of music or a particular dance, which can attract more people to the challenge.

Conclusion

Peer pressure in social media has influenced our youth tremendously. Naturally, people who are responsible, successful, happy people can be a positive influence. All in all, peer pressure is positive when it comes from people around you who are responsible, sensible and successful. is Therefore, the message of peace and other good causes can be spread among people all over the world by the help of social media and the Internet.

REFERENCES

1. Bulut, Serkan, and Topsakal, Taybe. 2015. "Support Movement for ALS Patients in the Context of Trend Theories and New Media Effects". Accessed at file:///C:/Users/Comp-/Downloads/343-356SerkanBulutTaybeTopsakal.pdf on 25 February 2019.
2. Haun, Daniel, B. M.; Tomasello, Michael. (2011). "Conformity to Peer Pressure in Preschool Children". *Child Development*, 82 (6):1759–67. Accessed at https://pubmed.ncbi.nlm.nih.gov/22023172/ on 11 January 2019.
3. "Ice Bucket Challenge". Auckland Northland Cancer Society. Accessed at Everydayhero.co.nz. on 30 September 2014.
4. Maxwell, Kimberly A. (2002). "Friends: The Role of Peer Influence Across Adolescent Risk Behaviors". *Journal of Youth and Adolescence*, 31 (4): 267–77. Accessed at https://www.researchgate.net/publication/251134155_Friends_The_Role_of_Peer_Influence_Across_Adolescent_Risk_Behaviors on 9 January 2019.
5. Rogers, T., Green, D. P., Ternovski, J., & Young, C. F. (2017). Social pressure and voting: A field experiment conducted in a high-salience election. Electoral Studies, 46 (2017), 87–100.
6. Reyniers, Diane; Bhalla, Richa (2013). "Reluctant altruism and peer pressure in charitable giving". *Judgment and Decision Making*, 8 (1): 7–15.
7. Organisation, A.L.S. "The Ice Bucket Challange." (2014): 289–95. URL: http://www.alsa. org/fightals/ice-bucket-challenge. html

15

Impact of Social Media on India-China Strategic Relations

Dr. Surendra Kamble

Introduction

The border dispute between India and China has taken social media to a new height and world's two most populous countries, China and India, are at loggerheads on the Himalayan borders. These two countries comprise almost 40 per cent of the world's population.

Facebook, Twitter, Instagram, satellite imagery and electronic and print media give real time information about what is happening on the borders at Ladakh between India and China. The names Pangong Tso, Depsang, Daulat Beg Oldies, Shyok river and finger area have become a household name in both these countries. The hypermedia and television anchors supported by the satellite imagery give minute by minute account of troop's movement and the strength of the two Armies, Airforce and their preparedness to the entire world on a platter. With media and satellites watching each and every move of the adversary, the countries cannot afford to tell lies to their citizens and starting war with surprise now is a thing of past as there will not be any cold start per say in modern day warfare.

Col. Santosh Babu and Ladakh have become a household name in the entire world. With social media and print and electronic media, the entire world is aware of the aggressive posture and the greed for some sovereign countries' land is apparent. Social media in today's time does not leave anything to someone's imagination. The expansionist attitude of China has been exposed to the entire world and no one believes that China did not encroach on the Indian side. Everyone is talking about the Galwan Valley finger areas Shyok river and the aggressive and expansionist China will be discussed in the social media for a long time.

Genesis

China draws heavily from two famous historical military books and Sun Tzu teachings. One being Li Guang (Chinese general of the Western Han dynasty) and his hundred horseman in 144 BCE and the other being, Zhuge Liang and the empty city in 228 AD. In both legends, the military commander faces a much stronger opposition army, but instead of ordering his men to retreat, he orders them to act in a manner consistent with baiting the enemy into an ambush. The stronger opposing army, uncertain whether it is facing a weak opponent or an ambush, then decides to flee and avoid battle. Military scholars refer to both stories to illustrate the importance of deception in warfare, often highlighting the creativity of both the generals' strategies.

The final teachings of Sun Tzu and Mao had stated in 1962 that China will not attack India and only by deception attack India following the proper teachings of Sun Tzu, which state that you don't use force to crush the enemy, but you use it to intermediate and then bring it back to the negotiating table.

China is still implementing these strategies of deception and is suffering the shortcomings of the ancient strategic concept. In reality, the deception by China just induces a greatly missed consensus of superior skill. China history is full of defeats and if the complexity and tricks of these kinds of literature worked, then, real China would not have been under foreign rule in most of these last 15 years as China had got its independence in 1949.

China has set a goal to become a superpower by 2049. Over the years, the world has witnessed China's growth chart and even sometimes got

US's approval rating. However, if you witness the relation between China and India, South Korea and Japan, it has seen downward growth from 2002 to 2009. China has been trying to push forward the concept of Pax Sinica (Latin for "Chinese peace") which is a historiographical term referring to periods of peace in East Asia led by China. The multiple periods of Pax Sinica, when taken together, amounted to a length of approximately two thousand years. Qiushi (a bi-monthly political theory periodical), the official publication of the ruling Communist Party of China (CPC) said that we must give clear signal to our neighbours that we don't see our war, but we are prepared at any time to go to war to safeguard our national interest. Beijing has stubbornly refused to fix past with all its 14 neighbours and their official view is that of the 14 disputes with neighbours of China, 12 have been resolved.

However, the Chinese claim is not true as the line of actual control can see China's creeping acquisition of gaining tracks of land with bullying patrols in Ladakh in water spring and Pangong Tso. Pakistan and China can act together in Ladakh 14 core borders. India has to face China in the Siachen Glacier and Pakistan in Ladakh region and their strategy is to cut off Siachen Glacier to Nubra valley and Daulat Beg oldie. Now India should also stop pleasing China and assert its own foreign policy and terms regarding Taiwan, Tibet, Hong Kong and South China Sea. India should not be overtly considerate to Chinese sensibilities and must do something covertly.

Battles

India and China have fought three Wars—1962, 1967 and 1987, in a nutshell the commissions are skirmishes. Skirmishes are as under the 1967—Nathu La and Cho La clashes also known as second Sino-Indian War or second Indo-China war where a series of military clashes took place between India and China along the side of Himalayan Kingdom of Sikkim and the Indian protector rate at Nathula and Chola.The Nathu La clashes started on 11 September 1967, when the People's Liberation Army (PLA) launched an attack on Indian posts at Nathu La, and lasted till 15 September 1967. In October 1967, another military duel took place at Cho La and ended on the same day. According to independent sources, India achieved "decisive tactical advantage" and managed to hold its own against Chinese forces. Many PLA fortifications at Nathu La were said to be destroyed, where the Indian troops drove back the attacking Chinese forces. The competition to control the disputed borderland in Chumbi valley is seen as a major cause for heightening the tensions in these incidents. Observers have commented that these clashes indicated the decline of 'claim strength' in China's decision to initiate the use of force against India, and stated that India was greatly pleased with the combat performance of its forces in the Nathu La clashes, seeing it as a sign of striking improvement since its defeat in the 1962 Sino-Indian War.

In 1987, the third Sino-Indian skirmish between Chinese and Indian Army occurred at Sumdorong Chu Valley, with the previous one taking place 20 years earlier. At the end of 1986, India granted statehood to Arunachal Pradesh. The Chinese government proceeded to protest. But the military movements in Tawang, taken in conjunction with this political action were seen as a provocation by the Chinese. In early 1987 Beijing's tone became similar to that of 1962, and with the Indian Army refusing to stand down, Western diplomats predicted war.

The result was a thaw. Indian Foreign Minister N.D. Tiwari arrived in Beijing in May 1987 en route to Pyongyang, North Korea. He carried with him messages from Indian leaders that there was no intention on New Delhi's part to aggravate the situation. The first formal flag meeting to discuss "the freezing of the situation" since 1962, was held on the fifth of August 1987 at Bum La in the aftermath of the Wangdung affair. Both sides decided to take up talks with renewed urgency and the following year, Rajiv Gandhi visited Beijing, returning Zhou Enlai's '60s visit.

Both India and China realised the danger of inadvertent conflict and after initial posturing the decision was made to de-escalate their deployments. The Sumdorong Chu fallout was that India and China decided to restart their dialogue on a new and more urgent basis. After Rajiv Gandhi's September 1988 visit, there was a hiatus of sorts because of political turmoil in India. But finally in 1993, the two countries signed an agreement to ensure peace along the LAC.

The agreement brought in an interesting concept of "mutual and equal" security where thinning of forces was envisaged, based on geographical and logistical considerations. However, its most important element is to have the two sides work out a mutually acceptable Line of Actual Control. As of now, the two sides have their own versions of the line and there are points, especially in the Sikkim-Bhutan-India trijunction, the Sumdorong Chu area and so on where the claims are disputed.

This is also the place where India claims the Doklam face off took place. Chinese think that it is part of India's policy to surround Tibet on the Frontier Sikkim. Their president even posted in the popular micro blogging site Wechat alleging that India's decision to move into Doklam plateauis part of New Delhi's plan to surround Tibet with Nepal and Bhutan as partner. The blog points out that India's so-called encirclement of Tibet began first. Doklam forms an essential piece to this theory and hence, China calls this New Delhi's Himalayan Grand Strategy. Now the face-off between India and China is in a plateau contested between Bhutan and China. While Chinese road construction affects the Indian claim over the tri-junction, Beijing contends that Indian soldiers are in Chinese territory—or, at best, in territory claimed by Bhutan. Because Indians are in a third country's territory, Beijing says that there is nothing to negotiate unless the Indian soldiers withdraw unilaterally first.

New Delhi may bet on a prolonged stand-off but the Chinese have given no inclination of being interested in continuing the status quo. But we must not forget that the bigger power is a loser in case a situation ends in a stalemate. Even China recognises that it can no longer humiliate India militarily the way it did in 1962 and it will suffer heavy losses for any misadventure, but a prolonged stand-off can lead to inadvertent escalation. Clausewitz posited this as friction or the fog of war, where accidents are unpredictable. The consequences of these accidents can often lead to a crossing of a recognised military limit, which would be catastrophic in the case of two nuclear-armed neighbours.

So far India has been mature in its approach to the stand-off, providing no provocation to the Chinese by any military movement or through its official statements. But New Delhi's position is critically dependent on Bhutan, a close friend and ally. Although Bhutan is unlikely to flip on its support to India anytime soon, a prolonged stand-off will lead to the strengthening of voices in the Himalayan kingdom who wants a more balanced Bhutanese foreign policy. In 2007, Bhutan had offered a swap deal to China where it agreed to give Doklam in exchange for the disputed areas in its north, which India vetoed. In 2013, the democratically elected Bhutanese government had started showing signs of independence from Indian guidance and New Delhi had let its displeasure be known in the 2013 Bhutanese elections.

India's next target will be Nepal so that it can surround Tibet, says the Chinese block on the social media post apparently as a comeback to India's popular string of pearls for encirclement of the Indian Ocean by China. Chinese police, defence and security forces say that Bhutan will soon become a second margin Indian state and consequently will be integrated with Arunachal Pradesh and if that happens, the middle and the Eastern part of the China-India border will be completely connected. This is a pensive if not merciful interpretation of the contemporary history and propagated by the Chinese intelligencia industry on the chat blog. A former consul general in Kolkata counters the exemptions saying that China is wrong as Tibet is not a problem for India and that the issue was resolved in 1954 through a consultative agreement with both sides with a joint statement issued during in 2003 during Indian Prime Minister Atal Bihari Vajpayee's time to China that India explicitly acknowledge that Tibet autonomous region was part of People's Republic of China.

Doklam

The Doklam issue then the widest part of the Siliguri corridor is now only 22.5 kilometres and it is called in India as the chicken's neck which means that if it was cut off, the mainland India would be separated from the rest of the Northeast state to a large degree. The Siliguri corridor has a strategic importance of keeping India's territorial integrity strong and therefore, India expanded its strategic space around the Siliguri corridor.

Are We as a Nation Scared of China?

Indian cycle right from the beginning has been made to think that China is a very big country and they are economically very strong and they can have smaller country like Vietnam, Hong Kong and China can defeat anyone with impunity. Indian think tanks are of the view that we cannot take or effort to have skirmishes with China and hence, all the so-called political class are in cahoots with the Communist Party of India and they have been made to think this. Many Indian generals have been pushing the fact that India should leave the Pakistan angle and focus more on China and the Ladakh region. However, we have had Prime Minister's say that even a blade of grass doesn't grow there; hence we should not worry about it. But now slowly China is showing its occupation in Ladakh. China claims Arunachal Pradesh from India which had been recognised as our territory by the British demarcated McMahon line between India and China.

In 1959, there was a brief corridor clash between India and China and Indian troops were killed. Then, Dalai Lama, head of Tibet, left for India and China accused India of sheltering Tibetan men and trying to teach China a lesson over the table. China has been considered more powerful economically, diplomatically and hence India cannot take an open fight with China. Our policies recognise Tibet region as Chinese one nation policy, Taiwan as one nation policy and hence, we played into the Chinese game. We are now facing a dilemma as Pakistan will join them from the west and we must be ready for at two front war on the land, in the air, under the sea and in space.

The China is facing US threat from the sea front when the two Aircraft carriers of US is docked in the south China Sea. All the littoral states in the South China Sea are having problems with the Chinese as the South China Sea is rich in minerals and there are a number of oil fields which can be utilised for their economic and countries' wellbeing.

China sees India as only a stumbling block in their becoming of a superpower and the only other country which can challenge China is the US which is 12,000 kilometres away and so the only problem is India. Hence, China sees India as a potential adversity in their becoming of a superpower, so economically and diplomatically, China does not want India to become an additional power, hence, they are in cahoots with Pakistan and now a days with Iran to keep India at bay. Following the string of pearls theory, China is acquiring ports at Bangladesh and Pakistan and investing a lot of money in Bangladesh. China has created a sort of chain around the entire Indian ocean to keep India's becoming of regional superpower in check. China is interested in the Indian territory of Arunachal and Ladakh and the significance of these ambitious designs is to become a superpower in 2049 which marks hundred years of independence of China. India is a stumbling block and they are putting roadblocks in CPC and BRI of China which aims to gain economic power towards getting connectivity to the European Union, Middle East and Central Asian regions. China also has fears of disintegration like the USSR and that's why to keep the Republic of China happy, Chinese always in League with their own people and they are banning the most famous social sites like Facebook and WhatsApp which is a total clampdown and they say that whatever you want you will be given and you will be given a good life, but don't ever try and question the authorities who is running the country. Chinese also want that Arunachal Pradesh should be with China, so that they could be connected from Arunachal to Myanmar and to the Asian region and completely secure the South China Sea and the

Malacca strait through sea as well as through Indian Ocean and have complete superiority over the 70 per cent oil route which is through the Malacca Straits in South China Sea. China also now hardened its position as far as Chumbi Valley is concerned which is threatening the Siliguri corridor.

China has always claimed that Arunachal Pradesh was being administered by Tibetan authorities hence it belongs to them as it is their own problem and which was also administered by Tibetan authorities and tax was collected from them and hence, the claim of the China. Major Relengnao Khathing, MBE, MC popularly known as Bob Khathing is a legend in Manipur but almost no one has heard of him in the rest of India. A student of Cotton College, Bob Khathing was given the King's Commission and joined the Indian Army during World War 2. It was Major Khathing, who captured Tawang for India in 1951, even as China's People's Liberation Army (PLA) was conquering the rest of Tibet. Backed by 100 bayonets of the 5th Assam Rifles, he evicted the Tibetan Dzongpons (governors) without firing a shot and planted the Indian flag on Tawang monastery. India awarded him Padma Shri (1957) and made him Ambassador to Burma (1972).

Peace and Tranquility in 1993

The peace and tranquility agreement between India and China was signed in 1993 where it was agreed that the truth will not be harmed and they will be resolved through bilateral talks. But the Chinese have always encroached on Indian Territory and scared away Ladakh patrols at the LAC. India is not recognizing that it cannot tolerate Chinese incursions and will have to identify China's weakness like economic power and tilt it in our favour. To strike them economically, India has been banning all Chinese apps which get a lot of support from the Indian market and India is also raising question of treatment of Muslims in Chinese territory like Uyghurs. India is now utilizing her soft power and hard power into smart power to do damage to the Chinese and we should not be unnecessarily scared of the Chinese economic superior. We have diplomatically beaten them in the South China Sea with the US openly supporting the Indian cause and other littoral states which face Chinese domination. The US has openly said that it will come to help any country whose over feels threatened by the Chinese aggressive posture in the South China Sea.

The first thing that we have to remember is that China has always respected firmness and powerand India needs to be self-reliant and economically and diplomatically strong. Hence, our ban on Chinese apps and goods through the Atmanirbhar Bharat programme is a master stroke. We also have to ensure that the encirclement policy of the Chinese being done through Bangladesh, Myanmar, Sri Lanka, Madagascar and Pakistan and Iran should be branded as of no use and India should build confidence in our population that we can do much more damage to Chinese then what they can do to us. China has also adopted propaganda against India with paid news to make public think that India is weak. Our aim should be to make our strike code more strong and our border Road areas has to be well connected. India also has to be firm about their territory and on the 18th of July in Ladakh the prime minister has clearly mentioned that no longer we will act like weak nation and the soil of India now will also exert diplomatic, economic and political pressure on China and will not be cowed down by their hegemonistic and expansionist attitude.

Strategic Importance of Ladakh Region for China

China has come all prepared to play a long haul on the Ladakh border because Ladakh plays an important role in its design to become superpower and create economically viable route with all important Central Asian region through China-Pakistan economic corridor and belt and road initiative. China will have easy access to the oil-rich Gulf region and an interrupted supply of the central Asian regions and the Gulf region and European countries so that their products can be sold out to all these countries without any interference and that's why there is so much of investment and creation of the artificial island as their military bases which China has constructed in the South China Sea region. China does not want their sea route to be endangered by any littoral countries. China has warned everyone to behave themselves and that's why the exciting Ladakh region plays a very important role in their scheme of things and if there Tibet and Indian province is threatened, then China's idea of becoming superpower will be a spoilt game and they will be disintegrated like the USSR. They want to keep Tibet and the Southern Mangolian province under their fold under an iron fist and hence, the importance of Karakoram Highway and the road which is being connected from the Karokoram Highway and towards the Guangzhou Peninsula so that they could have easy access to all their provinces and have access to them without any hindrance.

Chinese Intentions

India is currently leaning towards the US and China's intrusion in Ladakh has been a regular feature in the past. The present intrusion into the Indian territory is not a regular feature as the objectives of China this time around is that they want to occupy Indian territory and building a road through Daulat Beg Oldie. India is also not backing down and increasing its aircraft in the region and boosting strategy of airlifts where in the bridge over the river which is about 7 km from the LAC in addition to 36 more rigid networks of roads connecting to DS Road. The Indian soldier managed to reach finger point at the Indian claim line during last summer using an alternate route which is superior to China's. China's intentions are cleared and their decisions and actions are deliberate and not inadvertent trespassing. Their trespassing in the eastern most point of Karakoram range located about 8 kilometres south of Chinese border and 9 km Northwest of the LAC with the Karakoram Pass in the North-West is a strong objection to Indian infrastructure project even though they are on the Indian side of LAC.

The area between Karakoram Range and Kundan Range including area of Thana glacier is relatively important. Tibetans called it by Sanskrit name goes Thana, meaning a place for the cows, goats. Thana is essential to Chinese control of not only Western Tibet but whole of Tibet to maintain is game next 10 years after the state would come in from Arunachal Pradesh followed by Indian Ocean Region. Chinese think tanks have been making swap offers they are pressing India to recognise Chinese occupation of Aksai Chin and in return then I will give up its claim on Arunachal Pradesh. The famous article in the Times of India tells that from 80 years that they have been trying to settle the boundary issue and the boundary should have not been settled due to Chinese and Indians should maintain whatever is there in their position. In case of India it requires a Constitutional Amendment which is very difficult in nowadays with the fragmented strength of parties and hence the constitutional passing of the Constitutional Amendment Bill will not be that easy and the Chinese cannot have the glacier which is clearly mentioned in the Parliament that belongs to India and its Indian territory. The Supreme Court will also rule down the proposal and hence, no political party has this much of political importance or willingness to go against the sentiments of the nation. Also, now a days with media and electronic media and social media, politicians cannot take chances and they do not make any arbitrary decisions like swapping of the land or parting a piece of the land because there is nationalist feeling among the masses and no political party can afford that they their entire political game will be disrupted.

Chinese option in the coming days is to lay claims on Galwan Valley which makes access to Thana, secondly Gogra water spring areas and secondary access to Thana. Thirdly Ngari airport in Tibet will be 50 km closer to China. China can then cut of Indian access to Siachen Glacier by taking over Nubra valley with the help of Pakistan. The entire Pakistani army is currently sitting in occupied Kashmir and their planning to fly their aircraft to stations in POK and ready to take off, they should facilitate the proposed road connecting Tibet with Gilgit Baltistan in POK without Indian interference.

China has no option but to go to war. It has never learned how to face issues holistically and is also got used to challenge their neighbours. The problems staring at China are aplenty including credibility challenge, for Covid-19; diplomatic challenge for Sino-US, Sino-India and Sino-maritime neighbours. There is a PR challenge threat with Australia on trade.

How to Deal with China?

Whether China goes to war with India or any other country in South China Sea only time will tell. Till then the initiative has been taken by India to not disappoint them as they would keep coming back like a chronic disease. To deal with China we should consider these three principles of German Austrian politician Jal Von Metternich which states that weaker states cannot ill afford nearly to react to events and they must also try to initiate compromise which is the easy refuge of a regular or unprincipled man and hence, we must rely on execution of our plans on ourselves alone and on such means as we possess. Keeping the principal in mind the war should be fought by India and India alone without comprise and should not be restricted to battle front. There should be economic war as China takes pride in economic achievements and thereby controlling their population. Nowadays, the young population and students of China questioned the Communist Part of China and their thought process because they go to other countries for education and doing business and so they come to know what the CPC is dangerously trying to cut their freedom. The asymmetric war concept of nuclear, chemical, biological and economical disruption is in place and India should look at the disinformation and propaganda mechanism of Chinese operations of psychological warfare, technological and biological warfare. India should be self-reliant and develop technology, machinery and components and India should produce fertilizer, and all needs which currently floods Indian markets with Chinese products. China kept getting into India's manufacturing base and thus we should become firm as soon as possible and the Chinese economy should be given that jolt like we have given by banning apps and their losses of economy in terms of money is tremendous and that's why China has come to the terms and they are starting negotiations with India which they had not been prepared for in Ladakh region at least and they wanted to teach India a lesson and they had come prepared for a long haul. We should start neglecting the Chinese state-owned enterprises and have to back use of projects in India. The Chinese economic dependence on export was 19.5 per cent of the GDP in 2018 and that is the huge percentage to harass China. The confederation of all Indian traders said that it has finalized a list of 3000 products that can be easily made in India, reducing the Chinese imports by 13 billion by December 2021. 30 per cent of the Indian imports are technology projects and India should develop a strategy to produce these products within the country. India is also underutilizing their Steel and electronic and chemical Industries and this can also be ramped up with a roadmap for next five to 10 years.

Psychological and Disinformation Propaganda

China has much more to lose than India in relationship if it goes up in flames with India. They also indicate that there are forces between India and western country who are pushing the Chinese agenda through propaganda and disinformation especially the think tanks which are being paid by Chinese to depict China as a powerful and indispensable nation which has a major role in the progressive world. So this should be ruthlessly curbed by the Indian government. It is evidently clear that India can do without China and it would take some time but the future looks better and safe in addition to creating an economic roadmap within the country. China can be economically doomed if India will become an economic super power next only to the US and within the next five to 10 years it might give challenge to the US economy. Also information and propaganda are the oldest tools used to spread confusion in the enemy camp among the military personnel or civilian population and China has created a home-grown internet environment where nothing enters from the outside world. China has a firewall and the actual information cannot be passed on to public in China. India can target Chinese tourists and businessmen and students who study in foreign universities flood them with actual information about the atrocities by the Chinese government.

India's Response

China has been pursuing expressionist design for a long time now being a communist country analyst believes expansionism is crucial to its ideology now the India should also turn the table around. It should not submit to China's design and the role of India is to bind all our neighbours so that they could stand up against Chinese hegemonistic ideas. Now this has to be done very subtly and India has to become atmanirbhar to do this and keep economic sanctions on trade with China within the favourable condition of Indian and they should start manufacturing and investing in the neighbouring countries. China is trying to increase its influence in Asia and that's why they have started investing in Bangladesh, Sri Lanka, Iran and Pakistan. China plans a long term investment and that's why it has taken the infrastructure development especially the sea port to have a much bigger role in Indian Ocean Region. A leadership role in the Indian Ocean region and its economy to go hand in hand as that's where that 70 per cent of the all natural and oil passes through Malacca strait. China does not want to lose its hold over its neighbours and that's why has always provided subsidies to neighbours and always threatened them that they should depend on China and they should not ask for any other nation which is quite far off from them for favours and trade. China's military might is ranked third behind the US and Russia. 2.8 million is strength of its army personnel.

Chinese Perspective

In pursuit of centrality in international politics, China's primary strategic goal is accumulation of comprehensive National power defined by economic, military, technological and diplomatic global leadership. To attain this objective, it has long drawn strategies, firstly to ensure the domination of the Chinese Communist Party to retain distinct internal political and social code, secondly achieve high economic growth complemented by disciplined domestic environment, thirdly following the concept of specifying the periphery by deepening economic ties with the Asian nations to reduce regional tensions and finally Chinese intention to cement its international status as a central actor in the international arena as a prelude to its global influence in future.

South China Sea has become relevant for 80 per cent of its energy requirement and China is dependent on oil imports from middle east to keep its medicine supply route open and that's why China has always been looking for the Straits of Malacca rendering supplies susceptible to interference and Chinese has to secure it because of its economic compulsions and China have to dominate Indian ocean region and that's why Chinese plan of Pearl of strings. It is now eager to establish China Pakistan economic corridor and the belt and Road initiative is to develop strategic communication. Sino-Indian rivalry is a mixture of hard and soft policy characterized as India after the disintegration of Soviet Union, got closer to the United States to the extent of even forging a strategic partnership in South China Sea. India is the part that by its size and overall status judging a leadership role beyond the orbit of South Asia into the extended neighborhood and that's why China is emphasing on boundary issues.

The Art of War by Sun Tzu

China still follows the art of war. India does not want to lose even an inch of its territory. The standoff at the Daulat Beg oldi is in the focus because of its strategic closeness to 55 kilometre all weather road and that's why the Chinese are trying to attack patrols there and grab the post. The total mutual de-escalation of the two armies started after a series of bilateral consultation and we are in for the long haul at the borders with China and this time around we should not lose our focus. What is disturbing China the most is that they think that India will play into Tibet and Islamic region of Xinjiang province and that's why they are making Pakistan to pay their width and help China and help themselves by taking the Kashmir issue and liberating Kashmir and that's why Pakistan has given the air facility to the Chinese and Chinese have passed their aircraft in Gilgit baltistan area in POK. This is the critical region that China is currently constructing China Pakistan economic corridor and they have recently undertaken to build a dam. This explains the reason why China and Pakistan can cut off the Siachen Glacier by building the China Pakistan economic corridor and they cannot do anything about it because Siachen is the highest battlefield and the fighting took place in Ladakh literally so that the Indians should not have any thing on their side. The 73-day standoff in the Doklam area, including the finger four, between China and Indian soldiers, led to the both countries building new military infrastructure along the border of India. For example they constructed road and bridges to improve its connectivity and so since then both sides have accused the other of deliberately crossing the border on numerous occasions. India is at diplomatically and internationally advantage than China and this time around India should not lose even an inch so that Chinese could be taught a lesson.

How China has lost a friend in Ladakh and Chinese Deception

Post-COVID-19 China is facing great internal difficulties then why is it picking up fights with most of the nations especially with Narendra Modi, who had starting peace talks. Narendra Modi interacted with the Indian troops and said India can go about their lives peacefully because they know that our armed forces are standing there and protecting the country. For Beijing, the situation has taken unexpected turn as the communist leadership could not realise that PM Modi could take retaliatory measures like banning of their all apps and their telecom industry and their partnership in infrastructure development which was totally banned and their import items were stuck at the ports. China did not think that India will take such a drastic major and the minister of Foreign Affairs speaks for 2 hours with Ajit Doval the NSA and China has been told that nothing less than complete disengagement of troops along the LC and de-escalation from India-China border areas will be tolerated. China has to return to status quo.

Using Social Media to Appeal to South Asian Neighbours

In foreign policy, Modi imbibed in ideas rather than ideologies. He has demonstrated a skilful approach to motivate public opinion through social media platforms. He is setting trends especially in the contemporary digital field developing itself as a power that takes responsibility, deconstruction and to maintain global issues. His foreign policy is making India shine focusing on three dimensional objectives – economics; political and cultural. His main concern or vision is focused on strengthening economic independence in India. He is exploring bilateral relations with countries those were never part of India's international relations plans or ones where relations were too strained to move ahead. He has rebranded India's "Look East" policy as "Act East" with special emphasis on strengthening economic and security ties with Asian neighbors. Behind his vision is to develop or improve internal ties with key actors (especially East Asian) to increase global standing and influence for India. He used to communicate by tweets in their official language to connect the leaders and the people.

Survey Conducted

Nowadays social media is an essential part of life of users who know how to use the medium for various purposes. We have conducted a pilot study about the use of social media by students, researchers, faculty members etc. We have developed a structured questionnaire for this purpose and to test these questions from these users, a pilot study was conducted. To knows the views of various stakeholders who are using social media and social media tools, about the use of social media and its impact on Indian Foreign Policy, a structured questionnaire was developed and distributed to 550 participants which includes post graduate students, research scholars, defence officers, faculty members etc. Out of which we have received 484 responses from various groups of stakeholders.

A question was also asked about China playing an important role in international power politics and how it is not actively involved on social media. However, 11 respondents said that it is actively involved social media whereas 10 participants said it is not. Nine respondents did not respond to this question. Some comments on this question are that even China plays an important role in international power politics, however, they do not expose itself or any information on social media which is an external step towards success, China tends to be self-sufficient by having their own social media sites. China has their own social media tools for domestic use and China is developing its human resources focus on technology which is used by social media, but the information provided is limited.

It was asked whether strategic think tanks influence foreign policy through social media. 14 participants replied positively yes whereas 11 participants replied negatively. Think Tanks work on the agenda of the government and think tanks give out performance views and not necessarily what is good for the government. Participants were asked whether they were aware of the Indo-China border dispute, to which 22 replied yes, three said no and five did not respond to the question. The participants were further asked if issues raising this issue on social media influenced policy makers, following were some of the answers:

1. Through social media, people raised their voice to support government. The support of the people boosts the government in forming a policy in this respect.
2. Indo-China border dispute and Doklam issue on social media raised the issue to policy maker and hence it influenced India's foreign policy.
3. The media is not concerned about the border dispute as people from Arunachal Pradesh are under special protection.
4. It is suggested that academic community and intelligent researchers must come forward with such issues and find out solutions.

From the above comments from the participants, it appears that social media is mostly used to support the government or raise a few social issues which can be general, national and international. China is a developed country from Asia and is playing an important role in international power politics and helping Pakistan at various new projects. This question was asked to know the opinions of the participants that even though China is playing an important role in international power politics, whether China is not actively involved on social media. Out of 483 participants, 177 participants (36.64 per cent) said that China is actively involved on social media whereas 181 participants (37 per cent) said that it is not. It seems from the responses that marginal respondents say China is not actively involved on social media.

As per the report of eMarketer, there are three popular applications, they are WeChat, QQ and Weibo are most popular applications used by the users in China. There are 500 million active users in China of WeChat app in 2017. QQ application was launched 18 years ago even though it was the largest social app in China; recently it was rebranded to focus on entertainment among China's youth. Weibo app is called China's twitter, there are 340 million active users of Twitter with the key reason that this growth was the evolution of the service into a multimedia blogging platform with similar features of Twitter, Pinterest and Tumbir combined. Younger Chinese more aware of negative impact of social media. WeChat remains the most popular social app, while Weibo makes a come-back with younger users.

According to Kantar Report on social media found that Chinese respondents are generally happy with changes brought by social media. Social media give score impact on their lives is 79.8 but as compared with other age groups, people born in 1990s showed more caution against negative impact of social media. China has disrupted censorship drive on Whatsapp. It has been accessible through virtual private networks (VPNs) only, but some of them are blocked.

The opinions expressed by the participants are as follows:

- There is direct control of the Chinese government on social media that is why people are unable to express their views on social media.
- To some extent Chinese government is active on social media; it regulates censors and uses it for the party's interest.
- Chinese government policy is not that open to the world, they are very cautious.
- China does not get involved itself on social media because many social media sites are banned in China, they have adopted aggressive foreign policy.
- China is most emerging country after USA, China try to create dominance not on Asia but over the world. Today it is not possible to be powerful nation without social media.
- China has its own social media networking; their social media platforms are a little bit different from other countries.
- China has its own influence in the Asia to build one belt road initiate via string of pearls policy to connect every part to whole.
- Chinese social media is active but it is clearly dominated by their security agencies.
- Chinese companies are making a global reach as per recent activities.
- China has restricted many social media tools like facebook, etc.

It was asked to the participants if they agree that strategic think tanks influence foreign policies through social media. Out of 483 participants, 227 participants (47 per cent) opined that they agree with the statement, however 146 participants (30 per cent) participants do not agree with this statement, where as110 participants (23 per cent) did not reply to this question.

Some of the important views provided by participants are given here:

- As the riots happened between any of the religion or caste, it directly circulated through social media tools, networking sites or news and it influences the foreign policy
- Ruling party has their own think tanks that provide information to the ruling party which influence our policy.
- Data available on social media provides an insight into the opinions of the public with regards to the situation without actually taking into account the level of competence of the respondents.
- Because of the bureaucrats as political houses are at a loss when it comes to heavy subject like foreign policy. Hence, the role of these academic think tanks are important, sometimes they are a part of the advisory board of the nation.
- Strategic think tanks derive opinions from various state of society and analyse them and forward them to the government agencies or policy makers for consideration.
- Strategic think tanks do influence foreign policies but most of the time they are not too open on social media and maintain distance from it.
- Almost all the think tanks have their Facebook or Instagram, Linkedin, Twitter account which regularly publish events/ academic articles that shape/reshape the perception of the people involved in foreign policy making.
- Strategic think tanks give in-depth analysis as they are the best source, articles delivered by the scholars of think tank helps in opinion forming.
- Strategic think tanks used to shape minds of people as well as policymakers for any critical decision they gives advice to government. E.g. IDSA helps govt. in foreign policy making,
- The people in think tank are great minds and have lots of experience than the people on social media.

- They are an important stakeholder while taking decision on foreign policy in the nation's interest and national interest is directly connected with the people, since people of the country have a connection with social media, logically think tanks influence foreign policy through social media.

Think tanks provide their publications, research work online. As a result the information is able to reach a good number of people and this shapes public opinion, for decision making for people and in turn dictates how foreign policy is formed.

CHINESE FOREIGN POLICY

Introduction

In recent years, the relationship between the media and the foreign policy-making process in China has become more interactive and even a typical symbiosis. Though very conservative, Chinese media gives narrative and agenda and narrows its down and shapes its foreign policy through decision-makers. Chinese media is strictly controlled by the Communist Party.

As a milestone of media convergence, the Internet is altering every aspect of politics, economy, society, and interaction among human beings. Moreover, foreign policy decision-making (FPDM), a traditional arena of elite politics in China, is also slowly becoming more and more influenced by the Internet in a networked world. The increased diversity, velocity and free flow of foreign policy information, has raised public attention to foreign policy issues. This, combined with the widespread public discussion facilitated by the Internet, changes the context of, and exerts pressure on, the process of Chinese FPDM.

Media right from 2000 BC onwards remained under the state's control where reports and articles and their writers were directed by the Kings and now the Communist party of China, which controls the media. The media in China has its manifestation by way of Internet, social media, messaging apps, Twitter and movies. The government can monitor all these apps and either remove the content or penalise the source through the 'Great Fireball'. China has the world's largest and biggest media populace. Alibaba and its subsidiaries support the government agenda and gain financial support from the government. Any adverse propaganda harming the Chinese interest is curbed ruthlessly. The 'Reporter without Borders' gives Chinese media abyssal rankings, free media is only on paper here.

The reportage of Tiananmen Square is still banned which students, intellectuals rose against the hypocrisy of the rulers at the helm of the affairs. Thousands were mercilessly killed and fair analysis still remains banned in China. China due to 'Open market economy' has to have relatively free media and its interest has to be protected in hegemonic communist China. China is the biggest in terms of media internet users and government has to feed them with their version of stories whether in Xinjiang, Tibet or Yellow Sea. Domestic media is rewarded by way of advertisements and government funding to the 'pliable media'. Media including social media, is constantly monitored in China. The Communist leaders are shapers of the agenda and its foreign policy through aggressive bombardment of information and so significant is the Chinese media that US had to call 'national emergency' because of the Chinese 'Huawei'.

1) Analysis: Chinese Foreign Policy

1.1 Socialist Foreign Policy

People within the U.S. understand their government dominating and incursive different countries. The U.S. government serves the requirements of the large firms and banks, which require to economically and politically management different countries to create profits. China doesn't have a capitalist category. As a socialist country, China ought no to exploit or dominate others. China needs a peaceful world so as to develop its economy and to trade with others. As party 1st secretary Hu Yaobang aforementioned at the twelfth Party Congress: "We don't station one soldier abroad, nor have we tend to occupied one in. of foreign land. We've never infringed upon the sovereignty of another country, or obligatory associate unequal relationship upon it. In no circumstances can we tend to get form of government."

China has diplomatic relations with one hundred twenty five countries, most of that aren't socialist. it's willing to measure in peace with different countries if there's mutual respect for sovereignty and territorial integrity, mutual foreign policy, foreign policy in every other's internal affairs, equality and mutual profit and peaceful beingness. How do these principles of socialist policy apply to today's world?

1.1.1 Middle-East

China has taken a powerful change opposing Israeli aggression and supporting the Palestine Liberation Organisation (PLO). China has opposed every of Israel's school of thought wars and needs the withdrawal of Israel from all occupied Arab lands. It terribly powerfully condemned the role of U.S. imperialism in backing Israel. The Chinese support the formation of a Palestinian state within the Near East. At a time once the Palestine Liberation Organisation was facing a brutal Israeli attack in Lebanese Republic, the Chinese gave $1 million to the Palestine Liberation Organisation to use for no matter purpose they selected. The Chinese government has long had a politician, a political candidate} Palestine Liberation Organisation delegation office in Beijing and has refused to with diplomacy acknowledge Israel. (Marxists on-line, 1982)[1]

1.1.2 Asia

The Chinese emphatically contradict superpower obstructions in Asia. They condemned the 1979 Soviet-backed Vietnamese intrusion of Cambodia. The Vietnamese proceed to station over 200,000 troops in that nation and introduced a manikin government within the capital. The Chinese allow solid political and financial bolster to the resistance strengths battling the Vietnamese intrusion. They have supported the recently shaped Amalgamation Government of Democratic Kampuchea and battled to preserve its situate at the UN. Their bolster of the national freedom strengths is being demonstrated adjust in hone, as the Vietnamese-installed administration faces expanded issues and instability. Similarly, the Chinese unequivocally criticized the 1980 Soviet intrusion of Afghanistan, and back the guerrillas battling for the independence of their nation. U.S. troops have proceeded to possess South Korea since the early 1950's. U.S. and other colonialist powers rule the economy of that nation. The Chinese have continuously called for the withdrawal of U.S. troops, an end to imperialist domination, and reunification of north and South Korea. The Chinese enjoy close relations with the government and communist party in Korea. The Chinese also oppose any other imperialist domination in the region. For example, they consider the Marcos regime in the Philippines to be a right-wing military government and they politically support the resistance forces there led by the Communist Party of the Philippines.

1.1.3 Latin America

Latin America continues to be mostly underneath the domination of U.S. imperialism, though the Soviet Union and its agent, Cuba, cause a growing threat to the region. The Chinese support peoples' movements and countries' efforts to stay freelance of either world power. Throughout the Malvinas (Falklands) crisis, China condemned land invasion. It joined most Latin American countries in recognizing Argentine sovereignty over the Malvinas and needed a peaceful settlement of the dispute.

In Yankee country, Central American nation, and alternative Central American countries, China supports the popular forces fighting for independence and democracy against U.S. imperialism. Some western newspapers according that China had sent government observers to the Salvadoran elections earlier this year during which a right inner circle came to power. In fact, China solely sent 2 Xinhua wire service reporters to hide the elections. China expresses its commonality with the Revolutionary Democratic Front (FDR) of Republic of El Salvador.

1.2 Global Supremacy

"The quest after political system by the superpowers and also the resultant international group action between them are the most supply of the unrest and turmoil within the world," Chinese Minister Harkat ul-Mujahedeen Hua told the international organization Oct four. The Chinese imply that the U.S. may be a old imperialist commonwealth that's well-known for its domination of geographic area, the geographical area and different elements of the planet. The U.S.S.R., on the opposite hand, may be a new and hungry commonwealth. It covers up its actions with verbalise "socialist solidarity" and "supporting national liberation movements." in precisely the last 2 years, the U.S.S.R. has backed the invasion of Asian nation, directly invaded Islamic State of Afghanistan, and instigated jurisprudence in Republic of Poland. On a worldwide scale, the U.S.S.R. is on the offensive, whereas the U.S. is on the defensive. The U.S.S.R. is that the main supply of war.

The Chinese oppose the aggressive actions of either commonwealth and oppose their competition with each other. for instance, the Chinese have condemned the commonwealth nuclear race. China requires nuclear disarming and has offered to eliminate all of its own nuclear weapons. Since the two superpowers management the overwhelming majority of nuclear weapons, China calls on the U.S. and U.S.S.R. to scale back their weapons, to be followed by reductions by different nuclear powers and ultimate elimination of all nuclear weapons. The Chinese additionally oppose commonwealth domination and competition in Europe. for instance, they oppose all foreign intervention in Republic of Poland—each Soviet and U.S. The Union of Soviet Socialist Republics clearly interferes on a bigger scale. They believe that things in Poland should be resolved by the Polish folks themselves in order that Poland will relish bigger independence. Over the previous couple of months, the western press has noted hyperbolic cultural exchanges between the U.S.S.R. and China. China has hyperbolic public criticisms of U.S. policy. The press speculates that there is also a thaw in Chinese-Soviet relations. The communist and Chinese invariably create it clear to the planet that they're against hegemonism and imperialism and need world peace.

1.3 Decision-making Process

China's foreign minister is often seen as the face of the country's foreign policy but his actual say in foreign policy decision-making is much smaller than in many other countries.

The Ministry of Foreign Affairs is not the most authoritative or influential actor in foreign policy formulation in China. Instead, a wide range of Communist Party organs and government departments, plus the military, may be involved in the process.

The one-party state's supreme body—the Politburo Standing Committee—has the ultimate decision-making power on all matters, including foreign policy.

Below it is a Central Leading Group on Foreign Affairs, which convenes on an ad hoc basis to deliberate on major issues. Its members are some of the major foreign policy actors in China.

The group is led by the president, who has direct oversight over foreign policy, with the vice-president as deputy leader. Its secretary general is the state councilor in charge of foreign affairs, who outranks the foreign minister as the country's top professional diplomat.

Other members include the heads of party, government and military departments that may be involved in shaping foreign policy. They include the head of the party's propaganda department and its international liaison department, which is in charge of ties with foreign political parties and plays a special role in Beijing's efforts to reduce tensions over North Korea's nuclear programme. Members also include the ministers of foreign affairs, national defence, public security, state security and commerce.

But some bodies not included in the central leading group can also wield considerable influence, including the party's Central Research Office, the National Development and Reform Commission and the Ministry of Finance.

The party's powerful National Security Commission, set up in late 2013, was also given a major role in foreign policy formulation.

That is a lot of voices seeking to influence the top leadership's decisions, and their perspectives and standpoints are often not aligned and can even class.

2) Media and China's Foreign Policy

With modern science and technology constantly evolving and with increased public participation in politics, significant changes have occurred in the relationship among the media, public opinion, and diplomacy. Media has an increasingly significant impact on diplomatic activities: public opinion has become an important factor in shaping the government's policymaking and the media play an important role in guiding public opinion and exerting influence on foreign affairs. (Chuanjie, 2011)[2]

2.1 *Public Opinion*

Like ancient media round the world, the Chinese media aren't exempt from the pressures created by the status of the supposed "new media," together with the net and social media.

Citizen Journalism: the net, photography, blogging, and different sorts of new media enable voters to become correspondents, news on native likewise as international events. The results of this national journalism square measure for the most part positive, because the growing range of discussions provides the creation of a better-informed public.

Increased Reporting: because the role of media is increasing, their impact on policymaking is dynamical. Chinese media have evidenced desperate to report on problems that the govt. itself has not determined its policy on, particularly once the media see such news as in China's national interest.

2.2 *Perception of Chinese Media Abroad*

Despite the fact that opportunity of the press is an issue for Westerners watching the Chinese media, the discussants concurred that Western popular governments should indicate limitation while evaluating the degree of restriction, given that this wonder is available in the West too.

Weight and Reporting: It is a typical confusion in the West that Chinese news organizations at times purposely abstain from giving an account of touchy issues. Western media regularly face comparable, if not constantly obvious, weights from their administrations. Chinese media apply incredible exertion to improve the opportunity of data inside the nation.

Worldwide Reputation: The Chinese media assume a significant job in forming universal impression of China. Remote media frequently watch the Chinese media to evaluate the circumstance inside the nation. For instance, how Indian media regularly refer to the comments of Chinese media to underline Chinese patriotism and hostile to Indian supposition. Thus, Chinese media must recognize the obligation they share for the impression of China abroad.

2.3 Challenges

The challenges that Chinese media face are not, in fact, very different from the issues facing media in the West and in other developing countries, panelists agreed.

International Reporting: Due to limited budgeting and resources, Chinese media agencies do not possess a strong foundation for reporting on international events. They are often forced to rely on reports from foreign media without confirming the accuracy of the information.

Market Pressure: The need to keep viewers and sponsors creates pressure on media agencies to cater to the majority opinion. Sponsorship and advertisement revenue are crucial for Chinese media, and these factors play too large of a role in shaping programming and editorial content.

The Chinese media moving forward should emphasize quality of information to better serve the public interest, while at the same time fend off pressure from interest groups.

3) Internet in China

From Bitcoin to YouTube, the internet has greatly altered the way humans behave and interact. This is particularly the case in China – the largest online community in the world where everything from online payments to shopping has been pioneered and taken up with gusto. While foreign policy may be thought of as being largely immune to this phenomena, public sentiment amplified through online social media channels is increasingly sculpting Chinese statecraft.

Recent examples of what has been described by as "tantrum diplomacy" show that official responses by the government are often echoed by just as bellicose reactions on social media platforms.

3.1 Huawei and Foreign Governments

One noteworthy recent example of this is the very public confrontations between Huawei and foreign governments. In response to the arrest of Huawei executive Meng Wanzhou in Canada, the Chinese government responded by arresting several Canadians in China. This diplomatic punishment by the Chinese government was mirrored by social media users in China that encouraged a mass boycott of both Apple iPhones and the clothing company, Canada Goose, as a response. This proved to be a major hit to Canada Goose, its stock price dropping by 20 per cent in the following days. (Griffiths, 2018).[3]

This was a response that was very much in line with government policy. Yet the fact that it came from members of the public meant that the influence was cordoned off from official action while still punishing Canada.

While such a social media campaign serves the purpose of the Chinese government, there are other examples where social media sentiment is forcing the hand of the Chinese government in a way that may not necessarily be in line with government policy.

3.2 Stockholm Hotel Syndrome

The breakdown in Chinese-Swedish relations a year ago was one such precedent. After a group of Chinese was expelled from Stockholm lodging, this generally harmless occasion caused an online tempest in China and wound up a standout amongst the most discussed subjects on Chinese web based life in 2018. As per one specialist on the Chinese web-based social networking stage Weibo, two hashtags, approximately meant "Chinese Tourists Abused by Swedish Police" and "Swedish TV Show Insults China", got in excess of 220 million perspectives, making it a standout amongst the most perused issues on the stage for the year.

Fantastically, the internet based life furore provoked an official reaction from the Chinese government. Portrayals were made to the Swedish government and an announcement discharged, blaming the police for fierceness and having "seriously jeopardized the life and damaged the fundamental human privileges of the Chinese natives". The planning of the announcement clarified this was a reaction produced because of weight from internet based life, undeniably more than worries for the wellbeing of family included.

What presented the defense of the Stockholm inn episode so educational was it gives off an impression of being one of the main instances of the Chinese government responding to web based life impact, free of any more extensive point or methodology.

So what causes this feeling of shock via web-based networking media, either genuine or fanciful? The issue is undoubtedly twofold. To start with, treachery as a chronicled story in China has a long, and much of the time, defended history. The feeling of bad form and mortification that was delivered upon China by Western powers all through the nineteenth and twentieth hundreds of years isn't just felt by Chinese political elites however nearly the whole nation. Having opium constrained upon the people, alongside unequal bargains and enduring unmitigated land snatches has genuine heritage, which slants discourse of occasions to make the feeling that the world is as yet endeavoring to curb and mortify China.

The second clarification for this online life wonder can be sheet home to the Chinese political framework. In a nation where articulation, especially of a political sort, is blue-penciled and exceedingly confined, the political class and the open appear to have gone into an implicit understanding with regards to remarking on these sorts of issues. The gathering will endure venting dissatisfaction towards remote elements that can't ordinarily be freely explained towards their own administration.

The majority of this may seem, by all accounts, to be another obstacle for remote governments when endeavoring to creating arrangements for overseeing relations with China. Notwithstanding, this can likewise be believed to be a chance. Calls to put more in creating online life channels would be very much paid attention to. Growing increasingly web-based social networking joins legitimately to the general population of China can be a chance to influence informing, something that up until now, the Communist Party holds a close syndication over.

4) Soft Power Influence Globally

Beijing is expanding its soft power influence in a range of ways, none more important than its growing influence in the Western press. As part of Beijing's attempt to exert influence in foreign affairs, its state-run media companies are expanding their integration with Western news outlets. The CCP has rapidly expanded its efforts to influence the discussion about China beyond its borders to attempt to suppress criticism of the Chinese government and mould international media to refer to China in a positive light. In 2018, Xinhua, China's largest state-run news agency, announced that it was expanding cooperation with the US news service the Associated Press (AP), declaring that the two news agencies had established broad cooperation in such areas as new media, economic information, and the application of AI.

At the time, the US-China Economic and Security Review Commission warned that Xinhua was rapidly expanding globally in an effort to discredit Western media outlets. The AP maintained, in response to a Congressional inquiry on the scope of the agreement between the AP and Xinhua, that Xinhua would not influence its reporting or have access to sensitive information in AP's possession. In the wake of Russia's interference in the 2016 US presidential elections, no US media outlet would subsequently agree to partner up with RT or Sputnik. Some US members of Congress were of the view that Beijing's influence operations inside the US represented a similar threat.

Like other powerful countries (including, first and foremost, of course, the US), China utilises aid, cultural programming, and the media to boost its global image. But for Beijing, the current influence offensive is on a much greater scale. Beijing can more easily shape global narratives through state media that reaches hundreds of millions of people around the world. It is pouring money into such outlets as the China Global Television Network, turning them into major global media players, as Russia did with RT and Sputnik. Chinese social media and messaging platforms have also spread globally, making it easier for Beijing to push Xinhua and other state-run platforms onto more social media users outside China.

Beijing is also seeking to shape media coverage of China by using state-owned media to train foreign journalists, especially from developing countries, inviting reporters from Southeast Asia and Latin America to visit China to participate in workshops and courses that offer an officially sanctioned view of Chinese foreign and economic policies. Recent purchases of local media outlets in South Africa, for example, by pro-China business tycoons are providing Beijing with direct access to target markets.

Pro-China business owners are donating funds to influence research institutes, universities and think tanks abroad. China's Confucius

Institute project, run by the Ministry of Education, helps set up Chinese language and culture studies programs at universities around the world, including many in the US. It appears to have been successful not only in promoting language and cultural studies but also in creating a climate of self-censorship at many universities around issues deemed sensitive to Beijing. A 2017 report concluded that the arrival of more than 100 Confucius Institutes in the US had led schools to self-censor programming about Taiwan, Tibet, and the 1989 Tiananmen crackdown.

All the more star Beijing think tanks are likewise being made everywhere throughout the world, some straightforwardly financed by the legislature and others blessed by expert Beijing organizations. No place has China been progressively effective in influencing research foundations and business associations than in Southeast Asia. In Thailand, for instance, the Chinese government office has built up close connects to a few noticeable business and social associations that, over the previous decade, have turned out to be standard mouthpieces for Beijing's arrangement destinations in the kingdom and around the district. The German government exacted that charge against China in 2017, guaranteeing that Beijing had utilized LinkedIn and other web based life to target more than 10,000 of its residents, including administrators and other government workers, acting like pioneers of research organizations and talent scouts, and offering all-costs paid treks to China and gatherings with compelling customers.

Numerous nations' burn through cash anticipating delicate power likewise. The test is to separate between generous kinds of social and political advancement versus more straightforward and conceivably intrusive impact selling and impedance. While numerous Western knowledge organizations are centered around Russia's data fighting, relatively few of them are probably giving a comparative size of assets to comprehend China's impact activities and how the nation is anticipating its delicate power abroad. One could undoubtedly contend that Beijing's impact activities are undeniably progressively significant; given this is China's century.

Notwithstanding punching over its weight in impact hawking, Beijing is additionally punching over its weight in science. Achievement in present day science requires establishments of advanced education, proficient specialists, and a ton of cash. Since China has all the essential fixings, it is quickly climbing the rankings of logical accomplishment. Aside from its accomplishment on the clouded side of the moon, Beijing has spent a huge number of dollars to recognize dim issue, make incredible advances in quantum correspondences, and become a pioneer in sustainable power source and propelled materials. In 2018, Nikkei and Elsevier found that more logical papers began from China than from some other nation in 23 of the 30 most dynamic fields of study. While the nature of American research has been reliably higher, China is nipping at its heels.

The looming prospect of a dominant China in science alarms Western governments not only because of the new weaponry Beijing is in the process of developing, but because of the implications for how else it may be used—whether for repression at home, AI development, or purposes of spying. Science may end up changing China, and the world, in ways no one is anticipating, but for China to be all it can be in the scientific realm implies granting its scientists an unprecedented degree of freedom to be all that they can be. That implies that President Xi and the CCP will need to ease up on the reins of the scientific community in China. Are they capable of doing that? It remains to be seen, but President Xi has already proven himself to be masterful at adapting when needed to accommodate new realities and keep his vision of an omnipotent China on course. Based on his deft projection of China's soft power, there is little reason to believe that he will not be successful in doing so. (*International Policy Digest*)

(5) Media Control by Chinese Communists: Special Emphasis Tiananmen Square

The Year of the Pig is replete with politically sensitive anniversaries: 60 years since the Dalai Lama's flight from Tibet in March, a century since the launch of the influential May 4 student movement, 30 years since the June 4 crackdown on pro-democracy protesters in Tiananmen Square. June 4, 1989, will be termed as the turning point in China. Here thousands of protesters especially students and intellectuals are killed in the brutal suppression of 'Freedom of Speech' and 'Free Media'. These unarmed civilian students and intellectuals were protesting against the economic policy of Communalist leaders amassing wealth and entire population facing the brunt of low employment, growth and high inflation and rampant corruption.

Then came intensified restrictions in Xinjiang in early July, 20 years since the party launched its campaign against the Falun Gong spiritual movement later that month, and the 70th anniversary of the founding of the People's Republic in October. Those dates often bring extra censorship even on less significant anniversaries, and regulators seem especially keen to preempt any potential expressions of dissent in 2019. On Jan. 3, the Cyberspace Administration of China announced the launch of a new campaign against vaguely defined "negative and harmful information" online. It is set to last six months and has already included instructions to the web portals Baidu and Sohu to suspend their news services for one week this month in order to "root out undesirable content."

As the various anniversaries pass, spikes in censorship will be tracked by monitors such as Weiboscope; localized internet shutdowns and travel restrictions will affect regions such as Tibet and Xinjiang; and arrests or involuntary "vacations" will be imposed on prominent democracy advocates, grassroots activists, and ordinary Falun Gong, Tibetan Buddhist, and Uighur Muslim believers. If the past is any indication, at least some of the repressive measures deployed and the jail sentences imposed will last far beyond the anniversary year itself.

Thirty years later, Tiananmen Square cannot be discussed freely in Chinese media, so strict is the Chinese control that is can be called the 'darkest suppression of freedom of expression'.

5.1 First iCloud Arrest

The 2017 Cyber security Law stipulates that foreign companies must store Chinese users' cloud data on servers located in China. To meet this requirement, Apple announced last January that iCloud data would be transferred to servers run by a company called Guizhou on the Cloud Big Data (GCBD), which is owned by the Guizhou provincial government. Apple and GCBD now both have access to iCloud data, including photos and other content.

Personal communications and information from platforms such as

WeChat, QQ, Twitter, and Skype have increasingly been used by Chinese authorities to detain or convict people for their peaceful political or religious speech. This makes it only a matter of time before foreign companies with localized data centers become complicit in a politicized arrest. Apple has already proved its willingness to comply with Chinese government demands that violate basic freedoms by removing hundreds of apps used to circumvent censorship or access foreign news services from its mobile store in China.

Other companies to watch include the U.S.-based note-taking app Evernote, which transferred user data to Tencent Cloud last year, and various blockchain platforms, which as of next month will be required to implement real-name registration, monitor content, and store user data.

5.2 *Financial News Frozen*

Chinese censors intensified their focus on controlling business and economic news—usually relatively openly reported topics compared with political or cultural issues—amid a trade war with the United States and slowing growth at home. Propaganda and censorship authorities actively intervened to suppress negative reporting on a staggering economy by suspending online portals' financial news channels, issuing regular directives to editors to carefully manage their coverage, and providing monthly ideological trainings to journalists at financial news outlets.

This year, censors have already told the media not to report information on layoffs in the tech sector and restricted the circulation of a speech by a prominent economist, who said the government had made serious economic miscalculations in 2018. As the slowdown intensifies and its impact is felt across a wider range of sectors, the authorities can be expected to tighten their control over the news and work to prevent—or even prosecute—leaks of negative financial data and analysis.

5.3 *Technological Advancement in Data Technology*

Reports emerge weekly of pilot initiatives in which Chinese authorities attempt to incorporate artificial intelligence and other technological aids into existing control mechanisms. The more benign examples include efforts to identify and fine jaywalkers, limit illegal subletting in public housing, encourage good manners on public transportation, and improve student attendance at school. Yet even these cases involve considerable restrictions on privacy, possible false positives, and enormous potential for abuse. And in other instances, similar technologies are being deployed for more obviously repressive purposes, such as censoring politically sensitive images on WeChat or identifying potential targets for forced re-education in Xinjiang. Previous cases have been experimental or limited to certain geographical locations. But as these advanced systems for social and political control are refined, and as the government proceeds with its plans for a national social credit system, centralized surveillance is becoming the new norm.

Conclusion

Every country tries to control the media whether its social media or free press. Chinese have the dubious distinction of controlling the media from 2000 BC and now the only vibrant Communist country in the world. The agenda is set by the media populace i.e., China and its pliable media houses like Alibaba and Huawei leading to US declaring the national emergency, plays and tows the government line. China, especially in trade war and hegemonic aggression to further its national interest like in Xinjiang, Tibet and Yellow sea had to control the media and feed to its populace what the Chinese line of action is which is righteous. It always supports especially in Africa, Asia and third world countries to spread its business interest and accordingly takes decisions based on targeted population in china and third world countries. China putting its foot down on several occasions in declaring Azhar Masood as global terrorist points in that direction. China as a member of the United Nations Security Council always calculates and entire decision is ultimately in furtherance of its foreign policy agenda. The Chinese are very concerned about its image being fed to the world and the classic example is 'Winnie the Pooh' which was banned because the main character looked like 'Xi Jinping'. Thus, the Chinese media advertently is being controlled by the Communist Part of china and its furtherance of foreign policy.

The border between India and China is not clearly demarcated throughout. Along certain stretches of its 3,488-km length, there is no mutually agreed Line of Actual Control (LAC). India, following Independence, believed it had inherited firm boundaries from the British, but this was contrary to China's view. China felt the British had left behind a disputed legacy on the boundary between the two newly formed republics. Nearly six decades have passed since then, but the border issue remains unresolved. It has turned into one of the most protracted border disputes in the world.

Not a shot has been fired across the India-China border since 1962, but the Indian media's China "war" never quite ended. Border "skirmishes" and Chinese "intrusions" into Indian territory still dominate the coverage of China by Indian newspapers and television channels more than half a century on. But a change seems to be slowly taking place. The Indian media seem to be finally accepting that China does things other than stealthily intrude into Indian land or plot strikes across the border.

The border issue remains a major concern, but war cries in the media are heard less and less. So finds a survey by a team of researchers at the Observer Research Foundation, an Indian think-tank that comprises retired diplomats, bureaucrats, other policymakers, academics and journalists.

In their survey, the authors analysed China-related editorials carried by five leading Indian newspapers—*The Times of India, The Hindu, The Indian Express, The Economic Times* and *The Financial Express*—between 2012 and 2014. The years chosen are significant because they mark the rise to power of the two current leaders of China and India – Xi Jinping and Narendra Modi. Not surprisingly, the survey finds the border issue dominating the editorials. But what is new is an increasing plea for mutual trust and closer economic cooperation between the two long-estranged neighbours. Thus, an editorial in *The Economic Times* said on September 20, 2014, "...minus the passion that television anchors bring to bear on barren wasteland, the border is the least of our problems". "While the border still remains a very sensitive issue for India in particular, the newspapers do not allow it to hijack all other issues...The print media's interest in China is expanding to cover its domestic issues as well," says the report, titled "Understanding China".

Even on border issues, voices are sometimes getting more realistic than jingoistic. At the height of patriotic outbursts, the Indian media generally ignore the historical fact that the two countries do not have a mutually agreed border or that they differ even on the Line of Actual Control (LAC). The highlight of the 2014 editorials, the survey found, was the desire for a pragmatic resolution of the India-China border dispute by the then new Modi government. That may not have been achieved, but there was clearly a lull in the high-pitched media attention on border "incursions". The other issue that was found to have dominated the Indian media's perception in these years was the rise of China. The overall view is still cautious but there seems to be a growing acceptance in the Indian media of China's increasing economic clout and its role in global affairs. That sentiment was reflected in an editorial in *The Hindu* of November 29, 2014, which said China was "too important to be ignored, and it is unwise to believe it can be kept at bay".

NOTES

1. Marxists on-line, 1982.
2. Chuanjie, 2011.
3. Griffiths, 2018.

REFERENCES

1. Vindaya Senadheera, Matthew Warren & Shona Leitch (2017), Social Media as an Information System: Improving the Technological Agility, *Enterprise Information Systems*, 11:4, 512-533, DOI: 10.1080/17517575.2016.1245872
2. Penni, Janice (2017), The future of online social networks (OSN): A measurement analysis using Social Media tools and application, *Telematics and Informatics* 34 (2017) 498–517.
3. Dahibhate N.B. and Patil S.K. Library and Information services using Social Media Tools: Need of the Future, *Asia Pacific Journal of Library and Information Science*. Vol. 3, No.2 (July –December 2013).
4. Bindra, Sukhwant S. (2004) Domestic milieu of India and foreign policy making process: a theoretical perspective. *The Indian Journal of Political Science*, Vol. LXV, No. 2, April-June, 2004.
5. Schulz, Kerstin (2013), Foreign Policy Involvement Matters: Towards an Analytical Framework Examining the Role of the Media in the Making of Foreign Policy. *Global Media Journal, German Edition*, ISSN 2196-4807, Vol. 3, No.1, Spring/Summer 2013.
6. Chanan, Naveh (2002), Role of the media in foreign policy decision making: a theoretical framework. *Conflict and Communication online*, Vol. 1, No. 2, 2002, pp. 2-13.
7. Mukherjee, Rohan and David M. Malone (2011), Indian foreign policy and contemporary security challenges, *International Affairs* (Royal Institute of International Affairs 1944-), Vol. 87, No. 1 (January 2011), pp. 87-104 http://www.jstor.org/stable/20869612 Accessed: 11-04-2017 08:59 UTC

8. Barton, William P. (1950), Indian Foreign Policy, *The Australian Quarterly*, Vol. 22, No. 4 (Dec., 1950), pp. 25-34, Published by: Australian Institute of Policy and Science Stable URL: http://www.jstor.org/stable/20633300.
9. Cui Zhang, Charles and William Meadows (2012), International Coverage, Foreign Policy, and National Image: Exploring the Complexities of Media Coverage, Public Opinion, and Presidential Agenda. *International Journal of Communication* 6 (2012), 76–95 1932–8036/20120076
10. Kapur, Ashok (1971), Nuclear Weapons and Indian Foreign Policy: A Perspective, *The World Today*, Vol. 27, No. 9 (Sep., 1971), pp. 379-389, published by: Royal Institute of International Affairs Stable URL: http://www.jstor.org/stable/40394547 Accessed: 05-01-2016 20:12 UTC
11. Tully, Stephen (2014), Social Media in the Conflict Between Law and Democracy Chapter, In the book "Law and Democracy " ANU Press, 2014.
12. Chatterjee, Manjiri Miller and Kate Sullivan De Estrada (2017), Pragmatism in Indian foreign policy: how ideas constrain Modi, *International Affairs*, 93: 1 (2017) 27–49, published by Oxford University Press on behalf of The Royal Institute of International Affairs.
13. Kapur, Devesh (2009), Public opinion and Indian Foreign Policy, *India Review*,Vol. 8, No. 3, July-September, 2009, pp. 1–27.
14. Rubenzer, Trevor (2017), Social Media and Foreign Policy. *World Politics Online*, Aug, 2017. DOI: 10.1093/acrefore/9780190228637.013.485
15. Wynton, El. Social Media in Japan: An Investigation of the Impact Social Media Has on Cyber-Security and Politics in Japan. Electronic Thesis, Publisher: University of Arizona.
16. Nurmi, Maria (2012), Social Media in Public diplomacy: Survey on the Social Media Communication of the Finnish missions abroad, Master Thesis, Organisational Communication & Public Relations Department of Communication University of Jyväskylä.
17. Baru, Sanjaya (2009), The Influence of Business and Media on Indian Foreign Policy, *India Review*, Vol. 8, No. 3, July–September, 2009, pp. 266–285.
18. Staffer, C. (2018). *The UN Security Council.* Council on Foreign Relations.
19. Areg Galstyan, S. M. (2017), *Inside Russia's New Foreign Policy Master Plan*. National Interest.org.
20. Danylyuk, O. (2018), *Total Control: Anatomy of Russian Media Influence.* International Policy Digest.
21. Elena Labzina, M.D. (2017), *State-controlled Media and Foreign Policy.* Washington: Washington State University.
22. Vera Zakem, P. S. (2018), *Media's Role in Russia Policy and Decision Making.* CNA.
23. Adan, A.M. (2017), *Influence of the Media on Foreign Policy of a State: Kenya and Britain.* United States International University.
24. Barnett, S. (2016), *The Tragic Downfall of the British Media.* Foreign Policy.com.
25. Macshane, D. (2017), Brexit's Impact on Britain's Foreign Policy. *Carnegie Europe.*
26. Williams, P. (2004), Who's Making UK Foreign Policy? *International Affairs (Royal Institute of International Affairs 1944-).*
27. Aday, S. (2017), *The US Media, Foreign Policy, and Public Support for War,* The Oxford Handbook of Political Communication.

28. Coban, F. (2016), The Role of Media in International Relations, *Journal of International Relations.*
29. Hallin, D. (1986), The Uncensored War: The Media and Vietnam, *The Open University.*
30. Herman, E., & Chomsky, N. (1988), *Manufacturing Consent.*
31. Seib, P. (2011), *The Al Jazeera Effect,* University of Southern California.
32. Shah, A. (2012), Media in the United States, *Global Issues.*
33. *Wikipedia* (n.d.), Retrieved May 21, 2019, from Russian interference in the 2016 United States elections: https://en.wikipedia.org/wiki/Russian_interference_in_the_2016_United_States_elections
34. Belkin, P. (2011), France: Factors Shaping Foreign Policy, and Issues in US-French Relations, *Congressional Research Service.*
35. Grant, R. (2004), The Democratisation of Diplomacy: Negotiating with the Internet. *SSRN Electronic Journal.*
36. Jazeera, A. (2018), "France: Macron's New Media Strategy", *Al Jazeera.*
37. Matlack, C., & Williams, R. (2018), *France to Probe Possible Influence on Yellow Vests.* Bloomberg.
38. Schmidt, C. (2018), *How France beat back Information Manipulation (and how other democracies might do the same).* NiemanLab.
39. Westcott, N. (2008), Digital Diplomacy: The Impact of the Internet on International Relations. *SSRN Electronic Journal.*
40. Chuanjie, Z. (2011, January), Media, Public Opinion, and China's Foreign Policy. *Carnegie-Tsinghua Center for Global Policy.*
41. Griffiths, J. (2018), *Trump is Right that China Uses its Media to Influence Foreign Opinion, but so does Washington,* Retrieved May 21, 2019, from CNN: https://edition.cnn.com/2018/09/29/politics/china-media-influence-intl/index.html
42. *Marxists on-line* (1982), Retrieved May 21, 2019, from Encyclopedia of Anti-Revisionism On-Line: https://www.marxists.org/history/erol/ncm-7/lrs-china-foreign.htm
43. Pew Research Center (December 12, 2012), "Social Networking Popular Across Globe." Retrieved October 6, 2016 (http://www.pewglobal.org/2012/12/12/social-networking-popular-across-globe/).
44. Loader, B.D., and Dan Mercea (2011), "Networking Democracy? Social Media Innovations and Participatory Politics. Information, Communication and Society 14(6): 757–69
45. Fuchs, Christian (2012), "The Political Economy of Privacy on Facebook." Television and New Media 13(2):139–59.
46. Statista (2019), The Statista Portal, https://www.statista.com/statistics/507405/uk-active-social-media-and-mobile-social-media-users/ accessed on 19/01/2019
47. *The Guardian,* https://www.theguardian.com/society/2018/apr/09/social-media-has-poisoned-us-young-brits-on-why-they-are-unhappy accessed on 19/01/2019
48. Kantar China Social Media Impact Report 2017, https://cn-en.kantar.com/media/social/2017/kantar-china-social-media-impact-report-2017/ accessed on 20/01/2019.
49. Chatterjee, Manas and Jacques Fontanel Ed. "War, Peace and Security "published by Emerald Group Publishing Limited, UK, 2008.
50. Ravinder (2014), Analysis of the Basic Factors of Indian Foreign Policy. *International Research Journal of Commerce Arts and Science,* Vol. 5, No. 12 , 2014, pp 142-152.

Index

*